A UNIVERSITY COLLEGE.
B BALLIOL—B' GROVE AND GARDENS.
C MERTON—C' GARDENS.
D EXETER—D' GARDEN.
E ORIEL.
F QUEEN'S—F' GARDEN.
G NEW—G' CLOISTER—G" GARDEN.
H LINCOLN.
I ALL SOULS'—I' GARDEN.
J MAGDALEN—J' CLOISTER—
   J" NEW BUILDING.
K BRASENOSE.
L CORPUS—L' GARDEN.
M CHRIST CHURCH—M' PECKWATER COURT—
   M" CANTERBURY COURT—
   M"" CHAPLAINS' COURT.
N TRINITY—N' GARDENS.
O ST. JOHN'S—O' GARDENS.
P JESUS.
Q WADHAM—Q' FELLOWS' GARDEN—
   Q" WARDEN'S GARDEN.
R PEMBROKE.
S WORCESTER—S' GARDENS—
   S" PROVOST'S GARDEN.
T MAGDALEN HALL.
U EDMUND HALL.

V ST. MARY HALL.
W ST. ALBAN HALL.
X NEW INN HALL.
Y THE SCHOOLS.
Z THE RADCLIFFE LIBRARY.
a THE MUSEUM.
b THE THEATRE.
c THE CLARENDON.
d THE OBSERVATORY.
e THE INFIRMARY.
f THE UNIVERSITY PRINTING-HOUSE.
g THE BOTANIC GARDEN.
h THE CASTLE—h' TOWER AND MILL.
   h" MOUNT AND WELL ROOM.
i THE CITY GAOL.
j THE TOWN HALL.
k THE GAS WORKS.
l THE BATHS, ST. CLEMENT'S.
m RUINS OF REWLEY ABBEY.
n OSNEY MILL—n' OSNEY LOCK.
o ALMSHOUSE OPPOSITE CHRIST CHURCH.
p THE MARKET, HIGH STREET.
q GLOUCESTER GREEN.
r THE MARTYRS' MEMORIAL.
s THE UNIVERSITY GALLERIES AND
   TAYLOR BUILDING.

1 ST. PETER'S IN THE EAST CHURCH.
2 ST. MARY'S CHURCH.
3 THE CATHEDRAL.
4 MERTON, ST. JOHN'S CHURCH.
5 ST. GILES'S CHURCH.
6 ST. MARY MAGDALEN CHURCH.
7 ST. MICHAEL'S CHURCH.
8 ST. MARTIN'S, OR CARFAX CHURCH.
9 ALL SAINTS' CHURCH.
10 ST. ALDATE'S CHURCH.
11 HOLYWELL, OR ST. CROSS CHURCH.
12 ST. CLEMENT'S CHURCH.
13 ST. PETER-LE-BAILEY CHURCH.
14 ST. EBBE'S CHURCH.
15 ST. THOMAS'S CHURCH.
16 ST. PAUL'S CHURCH.
17 ROMAN CATHOLIC CHAPEL.
18 BOULTER'S ALMSHOUSE.
19 STONE'S ALMSHOUSE.
20 BRASENOSE LANE.
21 ST. MARY HALL LANE.
22 MAGPIE LANE.
23 COACH AND HORSES' LANE.

24 ROSE LANE.
25 PEMBROKE STREET.
26 BEEF LANE.
27 BREWER'S LANE.
28 ST. EBBE'S STREET.
29 ST. THOMAS'S STREET.
30 CASTLE STREET.
31 FRIARS' STREET.
32 BLACKFRIARS' ROAD.
33 GAS STREET.
34 BEAR LANE.
35 LOGIC LANE.
36 ST. JOHN'S TERRACE.
37 ST. JOHN'S ROAD.
38 LITTLEGATE.
39 JESUS COLLEGE LANE.
40 PART OF COWLEY PARISH.
41 WESLEYAN CHAPEL.
42 BAPTIST DITTO.
43 INDEPENDENT DITTO.
44 BULTEEL'S DITTO.
45 TRINITY CHURCH.

Images *of* Victorian Oxford

Shuffrey's view of the Clarendon Building and Broad Street in 1915. The University police took over part of the Clarendon Building as their police station in 1829 and cells were provided in the basement. On the right, B.H. Blackwell opened his bookshop at No. 50 Broad Street in 1879.

Images *of* Victorian Oxford

Malcolm Graham

ALAN SUTTON

First published in the United Kingdom in 1992
Alan Sutton Publishing Ltd
Phoenix Mill · Far Thrupp · Stroud · Gloucestershire

Oxfordshire Books · Oxfordshire County Council Leisure and Arts · Central Library · Westgate · Oxford

First published in the United States of America in 1992
Alan Sutton Publishing Inc
83 Washington Street · Dover NH 03820

British Library Cataloguing in Publication Data

Graham, Malcolm
Images of Victorian Oxford
I. Title
942.574081

ISBN 0-86299-967-7

Library of Congress Cataloging in Publication Data applied for

Jacket illustration: Oxford from Hinksey Hill *by William Turner (1775–1851) (photograph by The Bridgman Art Library, London).*
Endpapers: Plan of the University and City of Oxford from A hand-book for visitors to Oxford. *Oxford, J.H & James Parker, new edition, 1858.*

Typeset in 11/13 Bembo.
Typesetting and origination by
Alan Sutton Publishing Limited.
Colour by Yeo Valley Graphics.
Printed in Great Britain by
Bath Press Colourbooks Ltd. Glasgow.

Contents

Oxford from Boar's Hill, a watercolour by J.M.W. Turner which was painted between 1835 and 1840. The artist's viewpoint was, in fact, above North Hinksey where a lively harvesting scene and two strolling academics provide the foreground for a glorious panorama of the city.

CHAPTER ONE

The Setting

It was said in those days that the approach to Oxford by the Henley road was the most beautiful in the world. Soon after passing Littlemore you came in sight of, and did not lose again, the sweet city with its dreaming spires, driven along a road now crowded and obscured with dwellings, open then to cornfields on the right, to unenclosed meadows on the left, with an unbroken view of the long line of towers, rising out of foliage less high and veiling than after sixty more years of growth today. At once, without suburban interval, you entered the finest quarter of the town, rolling under Magdalen Tower, and past the Magdalen elms, then in full unmutilated luxuriance, till the exquisite curves of the High Street opened on you, as you drew up at the Angel, or passed on to the Mitre and the Star.[1]

William Tuckwell's description recalls the verdant setting of early Victorian Oxford which was perhaps seen to best advantage from the hills to the south and west, the haunt of Matthew Arnold's SCHOLAR GIPSY:

Runs it not here, the track by Childsworth Farm,
Past the high wood, to where the elm-tree crowns
The hill behind whose ridge the sunset flames?
The signal-elm, that looks on Ilsley Downs,
The Vale, the three lone weirs, the youthful Thames? –
This winter-eve is warm,
Humid air! leafless, yet soft as spring,

The tender purple spray on copse and briers!
And that sweet city with her dreaming spires,
She needs not June for beauty's heightening.[2]

In 1892, Josephine Butler recollected that:

Oxford in winter almost resembled Venice, in its apparent isolation from the land and in the appearance of its towers and spires reflected in the mirror of the floods. . . . We drove out occasionally to the heights above the city, to reach which we were obliged to pursue for some distance a road which resembled a sort of high level or causeway (as in Holland) with water on each side. Looking back from the higher ground, the view of the academic city sitting upon the floods was very picturesque.[3]

At close quarters, Oxford was equally captivating and, in 1856, Nathaniel Hawthorne remarked:

How ancient is the aspect of these college quadrangles! So gnawed by time, as they are, so crumbly, so blackened, and so grey where they are not black – so quaintly shaped, too, with here a line of battlement and there a row of gables; and here a turret, with probably a winding stair inside; and lattice windows, with stone mullions, and little panes of glass set in lead; and the cloisters, with a long arcade looking upon the green or pebbled enclosure. The quality of the stone has a great deal

A cricket match in progress on the Magdalen Ground in the 1830s. Away to the right lies Cowley Road and the eye is drawn across the unenclosed Cowley Field towards the distant towers and spires of Oxford.

to do with the apparent antiquity. It is a stone found in the neighbourhood of Oxford, and very soon begins to crumble and decay superficially, when exposed to the weather; so that twenty years do the work of a hundred, so far as appearances go. If you strike one of the old walls with a stick, a portion of it comes powdering down. The effect of this decay is very picturesque, and is especially striking, I think, on edifices of classic architecture, such as some of the Oxford colleges are, greatly enriching the Grecian columns, which look so cold when the outlines are hard and distinct.[4]

Edward Thomas was fascinated by the walls of Oxford:

Tufted with ivy-leaved toad flax, wallflower, and the sunny plant which botanists call 'inelegant ragwort'. They form a trail from the villages, upon wall after wall, into Ship Street and Queen's Lane, by which the country may be traced.[5]

Another commentator, A.M.M. Stedman, was struck by the bustling vigour of 'the High' in term-time:

Here will be seen one man rushing home from a lecture to his luncheon, his arm full of books, his academicals flying in the wind, and his head crammed full of the newest conceits concerning Virgil or Plato. There are two dilettanti, sauntering gracefully arm in arm, followed by a pair of pugs or spaniels of the purest breed. . . .

Next come three fast men, in coats and trousers of enormous and alarming patterns, with all about them of the newest and most advanced style. They have spent the last hour in the stables where their horses are kept, and have been regaling themselves with beer and choice stories. As they 'swagger' along they leer and wink at every female who passes them, and are greeted with loud shouts from noisy friends in the window opposite, whence too comes the 'tootle-tootle' of a post-horn, blown by some undergraduate who considers this amusement to be the height of wit. Behind them race half-a-dozen boating men bound for a big lunch, to which, with its slang of the barge and the water, they look forward, after a hard morning's reading. . . .

Here, passing, are grey-haired dons, majestic and serene, and here young tutors, proudly conscious of their new position, intent upon impossible reforms, or revolving sharp witticisms for common-room conversation. There are the velvet sleeves of the Proctor, followed by his satellites; and there tradesmen who have been vainly making calls by appointment upon wary undergraduates. And so they pass, the ever-changing, never-changing elements of Oxford life.[6]

To the insider, Oxford offered quieter pleasures. Arnold Toynbee for instance reflected upon

The Garden Quadrangle at Balliol . . . where one walks at night and listens to the wind in the trees, and weaves the stars into the web of one's thoughts; where one gazes from the pale inhuman moon to the ruddy light of the windows, and hears broken notes of music and laughter, and the complaining murmur of the railroad in the distance. . . .[7]

The historian, J.R. Green, who was brought up in Oxford, recalled the magic of May Morning when

We used to spring out of bed, and gather in the grey of dawn on the top of the College tower, where choristers and singing men were already grouped in their surplices. Beneath us, all wrapped in the dim mists of a spring morning, lay the city, the silent reaches of Cherwell, the great commons of Cowley marsh and Bullingdon now covered with houses, but then a desolate waste. There was a long hush of waiting just before five, and then the first bright point of sunlight gleamed out over the horizon; below, at the base of the tower, a mist of discordant noises from the tin horns of the town boys greeted its appearance, and above, in the stillness, rose the soft pathetic air of the hymn *Te Deum Patrem Colimus*.[8]

Littlemore Court in 1902. This painting by Evacustes A. Phipson illustrates the fine group of town houses on the west side of St Aldate's below Christ Church. The house with the two-storeyed bay window was Alice's shop, the place where Alice Liddell bought her favourite barley-sugar.

St Cross Road and Holywell church in 1910. The pantiled and creeper-covered cottages in this painting by James Allen Shuffrey were still picturesque, but their roofs were thatched until the 1870s and their gardens had been truncated by the building of St Cross Road.

The age-old university city described by these writers was subjected to many changes during the reign of Queen Victoria. In 1837, Oxford was still a small city of about 24,000 people and, in spite of some early nineteenth-century development, building was largely confined within its medieval limits. Old properties had been cleared for college expansion and general improvements, but the appearance of much of Oxford had changed little and, in the 1830s, it was still possible to see drunken men in the stocks at Carfax.[9]

The traditional role of the city at the heart of a rich agricultural region was emphasized in July 1839 when the English – later the Royal – Agricultural Society held its first meeting in Oxford and the streets thronged with farmers and livestock.[10]

It was, however, a symptom of the changes to come that Oxford chose to celebrate Queen Victoria's coronation in June 1838 with gas lit illuminations rather than a dinner for the poor. Gas had been introduced to light the city's main streets in 1819 and provided a novel and striking way of demonstrating loyalty to the new sovereign:

The magnificent gateway of Magdalen College was surrounded by a crown tastefully wrought in variegated lamps, and its pillars were entwined with double spiral wreaths of the same, with the word *Vivat* beneath the crown and the initials VR on the side. The house of Dr Gilbert, the Principal of Brasenose, exhibited in large letters extending along the whole frontage, and formed with variegated lamps on a ground of gold, the words 'God save our Queen Victoria', with a crown and stars. The effect here was singularly fine. The star on the College of All Souls was extremely beautiful, and attracted universal admiration. On the opposite side Mr Ald Sadler displayed a superb crown and star, with the royal initials, formed in gas-flame conveyed by a leader from the gas-pipe which supplies the street. The device of Mr Spiers, a glory encircling a crown, also in gas-flame, was much admired, as was also that of Mr Slatter, tailor, a crown and the royal initial in variegated lamps, the whole embowered in laurels and oak boughs.[11]

Cornmarket Street in 1857, looking north towards the churches of St Michael at the Northgate and St Mary Magdalen. St Michael's church clock was given a second minute hand in 1851 and, for a few years, it recorded both standard time and local time, five minutes ahead of GMT.

Two years later, in June 1840, the Great Western Railway reached Steventon and enterprising Oxford butchers were able to buy meat first thing in the morning at Smithfield Market and sell it in Oxford on the same day.[12] A corporation fearful of lost trade and a University anxious about undergraduate indiscipline had resisted early efforts to bring the railway to Oxford, but, on 12 June 1844, a branch line opened from Didcot to Oxford. Crowds watched enthralled as

Those rampageous, dragonnading fire-devils . . . arrived at a sufficiently astonishing rate, and though gasping for breath and shining with heat, seemed to have 'turned not one hair' more than was deemed proper by each spectator, even after its long and whirlwind chase.[13]

The coming of the railway brought new advantages, particularly as the network expanded, but the initial effect was to destroy Oxford's great transit trade. Even by 1850, it was easy to forget that

Nearly a hundred coaches came every day to and through Oxford; that posting to and from London, and a wide district converged upon Oxford; that several hundreds of horses were here stalled and groomed and fed; that the now fallen Angel and extinguished Star were of themselves tributary towns within the city. The persons directly sustained by this transit trade counted by hundreds: the money distributed, as wages and for commodities, counted by thousands annually; and there was a daily process of distribution going on.[14]

Enclosure of St Giles' Field in 1832 and Cowley Field in 1853 made large tracts of land available for building and threatened the still rural environs of the city. G.V. Cox complained angrily that

Oxford's first railway station in about 1850. The terminus of a branch line from Didcot, this station to the south-west of Folly Bridge was used by passengers from 1844 to 1852 and for goods traffic until 1872.

The 'Cowley Enclosure' coolly, and cruelly, 'cut off forty-seven foot-paths', within two miles of Oxford (some of them leading directly from Oxford), 'substituting for them eight new ones!' Most of the former were connected with pleasant country-walks, and were in themselves pretty, natural, and winding; the latter, of course, were dull and dusty (as being merely foot-paths by the new road side), and formal as being all in straight lines. Cowley Marsh, where at a short distance you might wander about on the turf without the formality of a foot-path, was doomed to be inclosed, for the chance of a meagre crop of oats on its soil of clay.[15]

By 1868, the OXFORD CHRONICLE was reporting that new buildings in this area 'rise into existence as if by magic; in North Oxford, too, ornamental villas of a picturesque character (are) springing up on the Norham and Walton Manors'.[16] Very soon, there were 'interminable streets of villadom, converging insatiably protruberant upon distant Wolvercot (sic) and Summertown.'[17] It was no longer true that

The inhabitants of that University town dwell in grey and ancient houses, time-coloured, and with flavours of old learning still hanging about their massy roof-trees. In point of fact their lives are passed for the most part in flippant spick and span villas and villakins, each with its half acre of tennis-ground and double daisies, all so new that scarcely any one has had time to die there, though numerous people have taken leave to be born there, and forming in this ensemble an ugly, irrelevant, healthy suburb, that would not disgrace a cotton city of to-day.[18]

In the ancient heart of the city, redevelopment altered the whole aspect of many streets. The numbers of students matriculating at the University increased rapidly from the 1850s[19] and colleges embarked upon ambitious building projects such as the Holywell range of New College (1872, Gilbert Scott) and the High Street frontage of Brasenose College (1887–1911, T.G. Jackson). Also in High Street, the University acquired the former Angel Hotel and adjoining properties and built the new Examination Schools (1876–82, T.G. Jackson) on a large site extending into Merton Street. Oriel College laid out King Edward Street as a commercial development in 1873, causing John Ruskin, Slade Professor of Fine Art, no little distress when he first saw the new buildings:

The hoardings had just been removed, and I awaited the inevitable explosion. The Slade Professor paused, surveyed the squalid vista, audibly muttered, 'Damnable, simply damnable!' and strode on his way.[20]

The city, proud of the county borough status that it had attained in 1889, erected a new town hall in St Aldate's (1893–97, H.T. Hare) and many business premises were demolished and rebuilt. In about 1920, Henry Taunt calculated that thirty-six houses and shops in High Street alone had been replaced within the last thirty years.[21]

Most contemporaries viewed this change as evidence of progress but voices of dissent were sometimes heard – most notably in the case of the national campaign against the proposed widening of Magdalen Bridge in 1882. In 1894, the Revd C.H.O. Daniel, Fellow of Worcester College, was mocked by other councillors when he criticized the demolition of seventeenth-century houses in George Street as 'an act of vandalism'.[22]

In 1882, 'A Visigoth' denounced the 'indifference and bad taste' of Merton College and the Oxford Local Board which had despoiled a pretty corner near Holywell church in just seven or eight years; a medieval tithe barn had been demolished, thatched cottages had been re-roofed with pantiles and their gardens cut short by a dismal new road.[23]

In the 1890s, J.M. Falkner described the character of late Victorian Oxford:

Instead of being a University pure and simple, with just so much of town attached as was sufficient to minister to University wants, it has become to some extent a residential

Changing Oxford depicted in the Illustrated London News *of 13 June 1868. The Martyrs' Memorial (1841–3), the Randolph Hotel (1863–6) and the Taylorian Institute (1841–4) had profoundly altered this part of Oxford within a quarter of a century.*

resort to which a great many are attracted who have no ostensible connection with the University at all. It is not wonderful that it should be so; the only cause for wonder is that the attractions of Oxford as a place of residence have not been earlier recognised. That it is the most beautiful city in the United Kingdom few unbiased persons will be found to deny – many will say that it is the most beautiful in Europe – and when to its beauty are added its intellectual facilities, its easy distance from London, and the pleasant associations of young and healthy life, which have on most constitutions of themselves a rejuvenating influence, the great increase in its residential population is easily accounted for.[24]

A roof-top view of Oxford from Magdalen Tower in about 1890. The Examination Schools of 1876–82 are prominent and tram-lines run along High Street, but much of central Oxford seems to have an almost timeless character.

By 1901, the population of Oxford had reached 49,336, having more than doubled during Victoria's reign. Gerard Manley Hopkins objected:

Thou hast a base and brickish skirt there, sours
That neighbour-nature thy grey beauty is grounded
Best in; graceless growth, thou hast confounded
Rural rural keeping – folk, flocks and flowers.[25]

T.E. Kebbel was equally critical of the new Oxford:

Formerly, whether we approached Oxford from the east or from the west, from the north or from the south, there was nothing to mar the effect of the *Coup d'Oeil*, which was in store for us. We came straight from the woods and meadows into the heart of the University, and found ourselves at once surrounded by its colleges and churches, without having passed through any intermediate zone of modern brick and mortar. . . . Now, on the contrary, the visitor approaches Oxford through a fringe of suburban villas such as you may see at Highbury, or Camberwell, bespeaking the growth of a new world outside an old one, and little in harmony with the idea of Oxford which he carried away with him a generation ago. . . . Formerly, all around and about Oxford it was difficult to find anything that was commonplace. Now she is surrounded with it.[26]

Quiller-Couch, on the other hand, felt that it was easy to exaggerate the degree of change:

It does not follow, because Oxford during the last twenty years has, to the eye of the visitor, altered very considerably, that the characteristics of Oxford have altered to anything like the same extent. Undoubtedly they have been modified by the relaxation and suspension of the laws forbidding Fellows to marry. Undoubtedly, the brisk growth of red-brick houses along the north of the city, the domestic hearths, afternoon teas, and perambulators, and all things covered by the opprobrious name of 'Parks-system,' have done something to efface the difference between Oxford and other towns. But on the whole I think they have done surprisingly little; and I am certain that it would be ludicrously wrong to calculate their effect upon University life by mere computation of the numbers of red-brick houses or perambulators. Naturally these innovations loom large upon the fears of those who have watched their progress year by year. But for this very reason it may perhaps be worth while to listen to a reassuring outsider who remains of the opinion that the true Oxford still lies south of St Giles's Church, and will for many more years than we are ever likely to see.[27]

To him and to many others, Oxford entered the twentieth century still 'spreading her gardens to the moonlight, and whispering from her towers the last enchantments of the Middle Ages'.[28]

The growth of Gown at the expense of Town; the new front of Brasenose College in about 1895. Many town houses and shops were cleared for T.G. Jackson's building, which was erected in two stages between 1887 and 1911.

CHAPTER TWO

Academic Life

Dons

'But what do they do?' inquired – quite recently – a tourist, pointing to the fellows' buildings of a certain college. 'Do?!!!' replied the Oxford cicerone – 'do? why, them's fellows!'[1]

In the early nineteenth century the Oxford don was by profession a clergyman not an academic. In most cases they viewed teaching as an interlude of perhaps ten or fifteen years before their college offered them a church living and launched them into an ecclesiastical career. Tom Davies, Senior Fellow of Jesus, refused all such offers:

He was the finest judge of wine in Oxford – 'the nose of *haut-goût* and the tip of taste' – and could, it was believed, tell a vintage accurately by the smell. Joyous was the Common Room steward who could call in his judgment to aid in the purchase of pipe or butt. He refused all the most valuable College livings in turn, because the underground cellars of their parsonages were inadequate.[2]

Davies and other dons who stayed in Oxford were

Only partially associated in the undergraduate mind with the ideas of education and learning. Each college was then a close, powerful, and wealthy corporation, doing what it liked with its own, repelling interference from without, and, perhaps it is hardly too much to say, a little University in itself. The members of this corporation, as long as they remained unmarried, and unbeneficed, held their fellowships for life, and were practically irremovable. . . . In Oxford and Cambridge alone were found these ancient immemorial nests of life-long leisure, the occupants of which succeeded each other like rooks in a rookery, where the tall elms tell of centuries of undisturbed repose and inviolate prescription. Individual birds were very often laughed at, it is true; but collectively they shared in the respect which was paid to the system as a whole. . . .[3]

Few fellows were actively engaged in teaching or administrative duties and 'coaches' took on most of the extra teaching burden which had been generated by the Examination Statutes of 1800 and 1807. In 1866 the OXFORD UNDERGRADUATE'S JOURNAL described the popularity of 'coaching' among young graduates:

The occupation has doubtless great attractions. There is a pleasure in teaching others work in which you have gained distinction yourself; moreover, it keeps a man at Oxford. Many men are sorry when their University career is over, and this excuse for a prolonged residence in Oxford is seized on by many with eagerness. Again, it is a most remunerative employment. Some popular Coaches have as many as 30 pupils a term, which at the rate of £10 per pupil per term would bring in an income of £900 a year.[4]

One famous coach, W.J. Morris of Jesus College used his 'acting skills to rouse his feeble minded flock' and encouraged their efforts by agreeing to accept double fees if they passed and nothing if they failed:

Also he made them sign a contract that they would work in his coaching-rooms eight hours a day, neither more or less. To such men this was really a contract of slavery; and he worked it like a master of galley-slaves. He was hospitably entertaining me once with a tête-à-tête supper in his rooms, to which he invited me that he 'might show me some of his methods'; after a cheerful meal of oysters and champagne, we were stretching our legs before the fire smoking our pipes when about 11.30 pm I heard sighs and groans penetrating down

from the room overhead, and I asked him what it meant. 'They are some of my eight-hours gang, doing their time', he replied. In a few minutes there was a knock on the door, and there entered a tall athletic youth with a haggard face and his hair wildly falling over his eyes, who gasped out piteously, 'Please, Sir, may I go home to bed?' Morris looked at his watch and sternly answered – 'No. You have twenty minutes more to work before you go.'[5]

After the Royal Commission of 1850–2, the Oxford Reform Act of 1854 began the process of diminishing the University's clerical character. College fellowships that had been dependent on regional qualifications or family connections were opened up and more were available to laymen. Scholarship played a greater part in the election of fellows and Charles Oman later recalled his examination at All Souls in 1883:

The history papers suited me very well, as I was able to ramble round all manner of topics in ancient and modern times. My marked file shows me that I had a shot at the Greek conception of the State, the Roman legions under the Empire, the Anglo-Saxon conquest of Britain, the history of the Crusading States in the Levant, the social conditions of medieval Scotland, the Portuguese and Dutch colonies in the East Indies, the causes of the American War of Independence, and the claim of Napoleon to be the successor of Charlemagne. . . . There remained the paper of translation from five languages, where I found four of them easy enough. . . .[6]

A don's room; H.W. Greene, Fellow of Magdalen College, in his cluttered study in April 1903. The room is notable both for its books and for the profusion of walking sticks and framed pictures; electric lighting had been installed in the 1890s.

Most dons came to see University teaching as their career and William Warde Fowler gave a vivid account of the efforts that he put into lecturing:

For me it was impossible to lecture unless I could be sure of gaining the men's attention, and in order to do this I had to know the substance of my lecture and a great deal more that bore upon it, so that I could talk freely outside the limited field of my subject proper, and also keep up my interest in the subject as it came on year after year. For having once achieved a successful course I found it was impossible to escape going on with it, and I had to create fresh interest in my own mind by learning something more about the matter, which I could use for some other purpose if not for lectures. . . . The exertion to me was so great, especially in hot or muggy weather, that I often had to go home to my rooms and change my shirt and vest just as if I had been in a football match. I may remark that I never read my lecture, but had a sufficient amount of notes to guide me in what I had to say.[7]

Some of the lecturer's problems were humorously described by A.D. Godley in 1893:

LECTURE to be delivered at ten o'clock to Honours men, on point of ancient custom: very interesting: Time of Roman Dinner, whether at 2.30 or 2.45. Have got copious notes on the subject somewhere: must read them up before lecture, as it never looks well to be in difficulties with your own MS. – looks as if you hadn't the subject at your fingers' ends. Notes can't be found. Know I saw them on my table three weeks ago, and table can't have been dusted since then. Oh, here they are: illegible. Wonder what I meant by all these abbreviations. Never mind: can leave that part out. Five minutes past ten.

Lecture-room pretty full: two or three scholars with air of superior intelligence: remainder commoners, in attitudes more or less expressive of distracted attention. One man from another college, looking rather de trop. Had two out-college men last time: different men, too: disappointing. Begin my dissertation and try to make abstruse subject attractive: 'learning put lightly, like powder in jam'. Wish that scholar No. I wouldn't check my remarks by reference to the authority from whom my notes are copied. Why do they teach men German?

Second scholar has last number of the Classical Review open before him. Why? Appears afterwards that the Review contains final and satisfying *reductio ad absurdum* of my theory. Man from another college asks if he may go away. Certainly, if he wishes. Explains that he thought this was Mr.—'s Theology lecture. Seems to have taken twenty minutes to find out his mistake. Wish that two of the commoners could learn to take notes intelligently, and not take down nothing except the unimportant points. Hope they won't reproduce them next week in the schools.

Ten fifty-five. Interrupted by entrance of lecturer for next hour. Begs pardon: sorry to have interrupted: doesn't go, however. Peroration spoilt. Lecture over: general sense of relief. Go out with the audience, and overhear one of them tell his friend that, after all, it wasn't so bad as last time. Mem., not to go out with audience in future.[8]

In 1895, H.W.B. Joseph of New College confided in his diary rather bleaker self-doubts about his lecturing abilities.

1895 Friday February 8. Bad lecture at 10.0. I find the Republic increasingly hard to lecture on, as the freshness wears off, and I have no new political wisdom or knowledge on which to draw: I am afraid the men find the lectures very dull and confused. . . .

Monday March 4. Lecture at 10.0 and 12.0: the first fell flatter than I have ever felt a Rep. lecture fall, almost no one seeming to think it worth while to take any notes: yet it did not seem to me unusually bad! I do not seem to make any advance in lecturing, mainly I fear through poverty of ideas: and it is a very serious question if I ought to stay on here.[9]

Joseph's self-criticism was perhaps unfair and he went on to become a formidable Senior Tutor. University teaching was, in fact, becoming much more professional and in the 1860s for example, the introduction

A group of dons outside Balliol College Hall in 1886. The Victorian period saw the college tutor transformed from a temporary academic clergyman into a career professional.

of the 'Combination System' enabled students to attend lectures at other colleges, giving more scope to specialized teaching.[10] *At the same time, an increase in their numbers enabled dons to take over the tutorial role of private coaches and make this a distinctive part of an Oxford education. J.A. Symonds remembered the influence of Benjamin Jowett at Balliol:*

When I began to read for 'Greats', I took him an essay on some philosophical or historical subject every week. The work for this essay absorbed the greater portion of all my energies. I neglected everything, except my sentiments and fancies, for its sole production. And in a certain way, I grew mightily under the discipline. I used to wait with intense eagerness, after reading my composition aloud, for his remarks. They were not much. 'That is very good, Mr Symonds'; 'That is not so good as what you read last'; 'You have been too prolix'; 'There are faults of taste in the peroration'; 'You do not see the point about Utilitarianism'; 'That is an admirable statement of Plato's relation to the Eleatic philosophers'. I can hear him saying these sentences now, bent before his fireplace in the tower-room of the new buildings. I treasured each small word up, and somehow felt the full force of them – expanded their leaves – until it filled my mind and penetrated the substance of my own thought about the essay. He taught me, indeed, to write; not to think scientifically, but to write as clearly as I could, and with as firm a grasp as I possessed upon my subject.[11]

Similarly, Arthur Waugh never forgot the devastating criticism that Professor Charles Oman meted out to his first essay:

He had told me to write an estimate of Cicero. He waved me into an armchair, and told me to read it to him. 'Marcus Tullius Cicero', I began, 'was born at Arpinum on January 3rd, B.C. 106.' 'No, never', cried my tutor, 'under any circumstances, begin an essay like that.' And he started me off on half a dozen different tracks. What did Cicero stand for? Was

he a genuine politician? Was he a trimmer? Did he do good for the state or evil?

Begin with an epigram, begin with a paradox, or begin with a demonstrably false premise and demolish it. But never, never, start off with such a dry and helpless statement as that 'Marcus Tullius Cicero was born at Arpinum on January 3rd, B.C. 106.'[12]

There was a danger, however, that the don would become a mere drudge. This was the view of A.H. Sayce of Queen's College who deplored the effects of the examination system on the teachers:

It is painful to see men wasting their strength and talents which might otherwise have increased the knowledge of mankind, or helped forward the civilization of posterity, over piles of examination-papers, confessing that only the prospect of pay, and the necessity of a livelihood, would have induced them to undertake the dreary task.[13]

W.L. Courtney attacked the repetitious nature of the don's task:

The fatal drawback . . . in the tutorial work at Oxford is that every few years the don has to begin all over again with a fresh set of pupils. In order not to get humdrum, your pedagogue tells himself that he will try new methods – only to find that the old habitual methods are the best and most effective, so far as the pupils are concerned. So every few years the old weary round begins again, with fresh faces among the taught, but a tired and perhaps gloomy face for the teacher.[14]

Many observers felt that research and scholarship were being virtually excluded from the University, and William Warde Fowler, for example, complained that he had been 'under the everlasting necessity of making an income by routine college-work'.[15] *Nevertheless, the advocates of a research profession made little progress and research degrees in science and the humanities were only introduced in 1895.*[16] *Arcane specialism continued to be viewed with suspicion and*

The old order changeth yielding place to new; a High Street scene in 1882. The idea of the married fellow living in North Oxford came as a profound shock to the old celibate don wedded only to his college.

A.D. Godley wrote dismissively of 'the man who specializes on the pips of an orange, or who regards nothing in history worth reading except a period of two years and six months in the later Byzantine empire. . . '.[17] *Goldwin Smith, Regius Professor of Modern History, stressed the value of good teaching:*

It is easy to exaggerate the service done by writing a single book as compared with that done by increasing the general intelligence through the effective discharge of educational duties.[18]

The Victorian don had two potential distractions from these duties. The first was the burgeoning administrative work which Mark Pattison, Rector of Lincoln College, identified in his MEMOIRS:

Young MA's of talent abound, but they are all taken up with the conduct of some wheel in the complex machinery of cram, which grinds down all specific tendencies and tastes into one uniform mediocrity. The men of middle age seem, after they reach thirty-five or forty, to be struck with an intellectual palsy, and betake themselves, no longer to port, but to the frippery work of attending boards and negotiating some phantom of legislation, with all the importance of a cabinet council. . . . Then they give each other dinners, where they assemble again with the comfortable assurance that they have earned their evening relaxation by the fatigues of the morning's committee. These are the leading men of our University, and who give the tone to it – a tone as of a lively municipal borough; all the objects of science and learning, for which a university exists, being put out of sight by the consideration of the material means of endowing them.[19]

The second distraction arose out of the Royal Commission of 1877 which at last allowed fellows to marry. In the early years of Victoria's reign, 'The sight of a petticoat in High Street was rare. It seemed quite contraband. Even a Mrs President took her exercise in some private garden.'[20] *By 1890, the change was very evident to Mrs B. Batty at Oxford Station:*

One don was met . . . by two lively children who leaped up and hugged him round the neck – some years ago children were rare creatures in Oxford! Not so now. Two young girls too waited for another professor – girls were never seen at Oxford in old days, I believe, except at Commem. *Nous avons changé* all that since married fellowships came in.[21]

A.M.M. Stedman was among those late nineteenth-century observers who argued that married tutors' concentration upon their wives and families in North Oxford had affected the esprit de corps *of the colleges: more positively, however, he welcomed opportunities for undergraduates to meet tutors' wives and daughters since 'frivolity and flirtation at afternoon tea is better than beer and billiards and ladies are less dangerous than barmaids'.*[22]

Undergraduates

I gained for many years a good reputation as a Lecturer, as I can prove by the following scrap of conversation overheard in the Turl by my friend the Bursar. Two undergraduates were passing him and each other at the same time, and one meeting the other said, 'Hullo, what lecture are you going to?' 'Warde Fowler's.' 'What sort of rot?' . . . 'Not bad.'[23]

The undergraduate's perspective of the learning process clearly differed from that of the don. Some, like Mark Pattison, came to Oxford as zealous scholars:

I had come up all eagerness to learn. Having had next to no teaching at home, I exaggerated in imagination what a teacher could do for me. I thought that now at last I should be in the company of an ardent band of fellow-students, only desirous of rivalling each other in the initiation which the tutors were to lead into the mysteries of scholarship, of composition, of rhetoric, logic, and all the arts of literature. . . .

I was soon disillusioned. I found lectures regarded as a

Undergraduates at Oriel College in 1863. The University embarked upon a period of growth in the 1850s and the average number of undergraduates matriculating each year rose from 389 in that decade to 821 in the 1890s.

joke or a bore, contemned by the more advanced, shirked by the backward; Latin and Greek regarded as useless, except for the purpose of getting a degree; and as for modern literature, the very idea of its existence had never dawned upon these youths, none of whom knew any language but English.[24]

Thomas Hughes' fictional hero, Tom Brown, was also surprised by the lack of work:

Well, first and foremost, it's an awfully idle place; at any rate, for us freshmen. Fancy now. I am in twelve lectures a week of an hour each – Greek Testament, first book of Hero-dotus, second Aeneid, and first book of Euclid! There's a treat! Two hours a day; all over by twelve, or one at latest; and no extra work at all, in the shape of copies of verses, themes or other exercises.

I think sometimes I'm back in the lower fifth; for we don't get through more than we used to do there; and if you were to hear the men construe, it would make your hair stand on end.[25]

Another set of undergraduates might have been unpleasantly surprised if they had been given too much work. These were the 'passmen' who were described by John Corbin as social beings with a preference for 'anything . . . that is well bred, amusing and not too strenuous'. They came to Oxford from the best public schools, generally at the age of nineteen:

By this time they have anticipated most of the studies required for a pass degree in the university, and find little or nothing to do when they go up but to evade their tutors and to 'reside'. It is by this means, as the satirist long ago explained, that Oxford has become an institution of such great learning. Every freshman brings to it a little knowledge and no graduate takes any away.[26]

C.F. Cholmondeley was perhaps a perfect specimen of this class, attending New College between 1885 and 1887 and yet scarcely seeming to allow work to interfere at all with his busy schedule of sport and general loafing:

1887 Monday June 6

Beautiful day. The Schools began and I was one of 136 in for Greats. I went up to the Parks in the evening and practised cricket in a net with Marriott.

Thursday June 9

Very fine warm day though somewhat cloudy at times. We had Greek Prose in the morning, but I did not do it, so went up to the Parks before luncheon to see the beginning of the Varsity match with Surrey . . .

Friday June 10

Beautiful day. I went up and watched the Surrey match between the papers . . .

Saturday June 11

Beautiful day. Harry's birthday. We had our last paper in the morning. I went over to Woodstock in the afternoon with a college team got up by Harding to play against a crammer's.

Monday July 17

. . . I had a fairly successful viva of about twenty minutes.

Tuesday August 2

Beautiful day. We heard that Uncle Hugh had died yesterday. Nellie and I did some fishing and caught six roach. I saw in the papers that I had got a 4th class in my Schools, which was a nuisance. Harry arrived in the evening from Cairo.[27]

By contrast, Montagu Burrows – later to be appointed Chichele Professor of Modern History – displayed a brilliantly organized approach to learning:

St John's College from St Giles' in about 1900. The unknown artist illustrates the fifteenth-century and later buildings of an academic community which, from the 1850s, was in the position to direct the development of North Oxford as a middle-class suburb.

Worcester College from Walton Street in about 1850. The artist, J. Perkins, captures the attractive juxtaposition of eighteenth-century college buildings and surviving chambers from the medieval Gloucester College. Out in the street, Town and Gown go their separate ways.

My method was the simple one of writing as hard as I could during the Lecture so as to lose no thought of the Lecturer; and I often gave his words, when at all remarkable. If he was dealing with one of the great books of the School, of which I had already made an abstract, then my notes from Lectures occupied the leaf left blank opposite, and I always noted my own ideas as to his agreement or disagreement with the author. My method certainly suited examinations. I not only knew all my books thoroughly, but nearly all that had been, or could be, said about them. Taken in this way the course was a splendid one, and though many changes have been made in it, its reputation is as great as ever. It is still admitted very generally that there is nothing in the world like it for forming the mental character of the statesman, the clergyman, and the literary man.[28]

This evident enjoyment of the process was not shared by Andrew Lang who bitterly criticized

This habit of carping, this trick of collecting notes, this inability to put a work through, this dawdling erudition, this horror of manuscripts, every Oxford man knows them, and feels those temptations which seem to be in the air. Oxford is a discouraging place. College drudgery absorbs the hours of students in proportion to their conscientiousness. They have only the waste odds-and-ends of time for their own labours. They live in an atmosphere of criticism. They collect notes, they wait, they dream; their youth goes by, and the night comes when no man can work.[29]

In similar vein, Hilaire Belloc responded angrily to a don's dissection of his essay:

> Remote and ineffectual Don
> That dared attack my Chesterton,
> With that poor weapon, half-impelled,
> Unlearnt, unsteady, hardly held,

Unworthy for a tilt with men –
Your quavering and corroded pen;
Don poor at Bed and worse at Table,
Don pinched, Don starved, Don miserable;
Don stuttering, Don with roving eyes,
Don nervous, Don of crudities;
Don clerical, Don ordinary,
Don self-absorbed and solitary;
Don here-and-there, Don epileptic;
Don middle-class, Don sycophantic,
Don dull, Don brutish, Don pedantic;
Don hypocritical, Don bad,
Don furtive, Don three-quarters mad;
Don (since a man must make an end),
Don that shall never be my friend. . . .[30]

The undergraduate years led inexorably to finals and that stomach-tightening walk to the Examination Schools:

It struck him as rather odd and unnatural, in walking up Homonovus Lane, that everything should be going on just as usual. Breakfast-tins, dogs and walking-sticks for sale; new trousers, cads, hansoms – nothing in the shop-windows which seemed to bear on his anxious condition. Ford, the horse-breaker, met him, looked at him with his hard fearless face, and took off his hat, instead of touching it as usual in return to Hugh's nod and 'good morning'. The white tie impressed him, it seemed; at all events he said nothing. There was a group of pale men, also white-tied by St Mary's and a crowd in Schools' quadrangle. Some pressed close to the door of the Writing School, some seemed 'loath to depart' from the conversation of their friends, and chatted eagerly in the open. There were five minutes to spare, and Hugh revolved Dayrell's last advice: 'Don't lose time; look through the paper, and the first thing you see you can do, do it at once. One idea always leads to another. Nothing like a good re-echoing memory.' So he opened his Logic paper, ran his eye down it, and found he knew Question 7, and wrote it out. As he went on, he lit on a good beginning for No. 6; then he saw his way to No. 2 and 1. . . .[31]

For some, the tension was too much; James Pycroft recalled, for example, the case of Jones of Jesus College:

Jones was seen to look unutterable things at his set of logic questions, and at last he doubled up and emphatically creased the paper – walked up with a very determined step, and in a very depreciatory manner gave in the paper to us, and left the schools. When we looked at it we found it endorsed as follows:

'Mr Jones presents his compliments to the examiners and declines to trouble them any further on this occasion. Mr Jones would express due deference to the examiners as deeply thinking men, but he cannot conceal his unalterable conviction that logic is all a pack of stuff.'[32]

Failure – in Oxford terms 'being plucked' – was a dreadful fate:

Oh! what a misery is it to be plucked! One undergraduate was driven mad by it and committed suicide. Some will speak lightly of it among their fellow-collegians; for of course the idle and the shameless will everywhere find a few to keep them in countenance. But I never knew a man so bold as to deny that a pluck was a very sore subject at home. First of all, the very name of being plucked sounds in almost every ear as the just punishment of a brainless, idle dunce. The term itself is contemptible: it is associated with the meanest, the most stupid and spiritless animals of creation. When we hear of a man being plucked, we think he is necessarily a goose. This is the general association; not always the just conclusion, perhaps; for some few clever men and good scholars have been plucked; still public opinion does not change for solitary exceptions such as these.[33]

Hope and despair, elation and misery; just some of the emotions of the examination candidate depicted by George Davis of Oxford at the turn of the century.

A.D. Godley's poem ALPHABET illustrated a happier outcome to examination nerves:

A was the Anguish I felt in the schools,
B was my Bugbear, the tenses and rules,
C was the Cramming for months I had got,

D the Declension I knew and forgot,
E was the English to put into Latin,
F was the Funk that for hours I sat in,
G was the Grammar I never knew much of,
H was the Homer I hated the touch of,
I were the Idioms that on my brain preyed,
J were the Jokes the Examiners made,
K the Kind way they asked where Lorraine was,
L was their Look when I said it in Spain was,
M the Mistakes they against me were chalking,
N was the Nonsense I knew I was talking,
O was the Ode that I couldn't translate,
P was the Prose that shared the same fate,
Q was a Question they asked me in chaff,
R my Reply that made them all laugh,
S was their Smile which is haunting me yet,
T the Testamur I wanted to get,
U the Unkind way I'm told that there's none,
V was the Villain who said it in fun,
W was the Waiting – I never forgot it,
X my Xcitement at last when I got it,
Y were my Yells of uproarious din,
Z was the Zenith of joy I was in.[34]

The male undergraduate, used to competing academically against his fellows, discovered new rivals in the form of 'undergraduettes' as women gained a toe-hold in higher education. In 1866, some of the wives and sisters of Oxford dons gained permission to attend University lectures and classes and the OXFORD UNDER-GRADUATE'S JOURNAL hoped that 'in time we may enrol in the lists of Convocation, Spinsters of Arts and Mistresses of Hearts'.[35] Oxford admitted girls to the senior local examinations in 1870 and, three years later, Worcester College offered an exhibition to A.M.A.H. Rogers who topped the examination list. The offer had to be withdrawn, however, when the successful candidate was identified as Annie Rogers, daughter of Professor Thorold Rogers.[36] Her success led to an inevitable conclusion, and finally, in 1879, Somerville Hall

and Lady Margaret Hall opened their doors to the first women students. The first principal of Lady Margaret Hall, Elizabeth Wordsworth, recalled the primitive conditions that greeted them:

The draughts were fearful; the doors and windows all over the house were made of unseasoned wood, and the students used to say they could get charming views of the country through the interstices of their window-frames! The way the chimneys smoked was awful. It was, naturally, a pet joke . . . at our committees to inquire after the welfare of these chimneys; but it was less of a joke to us to find our pretty bedroom things fresh brought from home all covered with soot. Another tragedy was the black paint coming off the backs of the rush chairs which had been rather hastily provided, and ruining at least one pretty dress! We had a tiny chapel, afterwards the pantry, on the ground floor. . . . Our library would not have filled a single shelf. It consisted at first of exactly two books: a quite unintelligible Treatise on Sound and Colour, with (I think) coloured diagrams, which someone gave us; and a well-worn copy of 'The New-comes'. . . .[37]

The arrival of women undergraduates excited fierce opposition from conservative Oxonians like John Burgon, Dean of Chichester:

A new and hitherto unheard-of experiment it seems is to be tried in this place: nothing less than the education of young Women *like* young Men and *with* young Men. Has the University seriously considered the inevitable consequences of this wild project? . . . Will none of you have the generosity or the candour to tell (Woman) what a very disagreeable creature, in Man's account, she will inevitably become? If she is to compete successfully with men for 'honours', you must needs put the classic writers of antiquity unreservedly into her hands – in other words, must introduce her to the obscenities of Greek and Roman literature. Can you seriously intend it? Is it then a part of your programme to defile that lovely spirit with the filth of old-world civilization. and to acquaint maidens in

Women students of Lady Margaret Hall with the first principal, Elizabeth Wordsworth, in 1888. A lengthy campaign for the higher education of women had borne fruit in October 1879 when Lady Margaret Hall and Somerville Hall opened with just twenty-one students between them.

their flower with a hundred abominable things which women of any age, – (and men too, if *that* were possible), – would rather a thousand times be without? . . .

I take leave of the subject with a short Allocution addressed to the other sex: 'Inferior to us God made you: and inferior to the end of time you will remain. But you are not the worse off for that.'[38]

Others adopted a dismissive attitude, seeing the women as guests rather than as serious students. Congregation allowed them to sit some honours examinations from 1884, but refused an attempt to give them degrees in 1896. A.D. Godley felt that they ought to be pleased.

Ye Somervillian students, Ye ladies of St Hugh's,
Whose rashness and imprudence Provokes my warning Muse,
Receive not with impatience, But calmly, as you should,
These simple observations – I make them for your good.

Why seek for mere diplomas And commonplace degrees,
When now – unfettered roamers – You study what you
   please, –
While Man in like conditions Is forced to stick like gum
Unto the requisitions of a *curriculum*?

When Proctors fine and gate you, If walking thro' the town
In *pupillari statu* Without a cap or gown:
When gauds that now delight you Away you have to throw,
And sadly go *vestitu In academico*:

When your untried impatience Is treated every day
By rules and regulations: When academic sway
Your study's sphere belittles, You'll find that life, I fear
Is not completely skittles, Nor altogether beer.

His poem drew 'A RETORT' from C.E. Brownrigg:

You *horrid* A G! You unnatural man!
I don't like your verses *a bit*;

LADIES NOT ADMITTED.

" VERY SORRY, MISS MINERVA, BUT PERHAPS YOU ARE NOT AWARE THAT THIS IS A MONASTIC ESTABLISHMENT."

[" The lady students of the Universities have received a cruel series of rebuffs within the last few days. On Tuesday week the Congregation of the University of Oxford refused to admit them to the B.A. degree. On Tuesday last it followed up this blow by rejecting all the resolutions proposed as alternatives. Yesterday the Cambridge Senate inflicted the unkindest cut of all by practically imitating the ungallant example of Oxford."
Times, March 13 189

Ladies not admitted; a Punch *cartoon in March 1896. A conservative University still saw women students as guests rather than full members and refused to grant them degrees until 1920.*

Our JUST ASPIRATIONS you ruthlessly ban,
And this, Sir, you fancy is wit!

I scorn your contempt, and disdain your advice;
I don't see your logical *ergo*;
And though I could be most uncommonly nice,
I am now most *indignantly* Virgo.[39]

For all the patronizing, it became obvious to many male under-graduates that women were – at least – their intellectual equals:

In spite of long hours with a crammer
I never got more than a Gamma,
But the girl over there
With the flaming red hair
Gets Alpha Plus every time, damn her![40]

Benjamin Jowett, Master of Balliol College, surprised outside the college in about 1890 when talking to Henry Acland (left) and Dr H.G. Woods, President of Trinity College (right). Jowett was very reluctant to have his photograph taken and Henry Taunt was delighted to have 'captured' him.

CHAPTER THREE

Varsity Characters

First come I: My name is *Jowett*:
Whatever can be known I know it
I am the Master of the College
What I know not is not knowledge.

I'm the self-distinguishing
Consciousness in everything;
The synthetic unity,
One in multiplicity,
The unseen nexus of the seen,
Sometimes known as Tommy *Green*.

So to say – at least, you know,
I am *Nettleship*, or so;
Or, in other words, I mean
What they call the Junior Dean.
You are gated after Hall:
That's all; at least – that's nearly all.'[1]

Victorian Oxford was full of 'characters', some noted for their intellectual or other achievements and others perhaps better known for their eccentricity. Some of these individuals shone brightly on the local scene but are now largely forgotten: not a few, however, achieved and retain a world-wide reputation.

Some of Oxford's heads of houses were particularly notable. Dr John Routh was 100 years old when he died in 1854, having been President of Magdalen College since 1791:

It was as a *spectacle* that he excited popular interest; to see him shuffle into Chapel from his lodgings a Sunday crowd assembled. The wig, with trencher cap insecurely poised above it, the long cassock, ample gown, shorts and buckled shoes; the bent form, pale venerable face, enormous pendent eyebrows, generic to antique portraits in Bodleian gallery or College Halls, were here to be seen alive –

Some statue you would swear
Stepped from its pedestal to take the air.

His wife was scarcely less noticeable:

She was born in the year of his election to the presidency, 1791; so that between 'her dear man', as she called him, and herself – 'that crathy old woman', as *he* occasionally called *her* – were nearly forty years. But she had become rapidly and prematurely old: with strongly marked features, a large moustache, and a profusion of grey hair, she paraded the streets, a spectral figure, in a little chaise drawn by a donkey and attended by a hunchbacked lad named Cox. 'Woman', her husband would say to her, when from the luncheon table he saw Cox leading the donkey carriage round, 'Woman, the ass is at the door.'[2]

Benjamin Jowett, Master of Balliol from 1870 until his death in 1893, became a dominant force, feared but respected by his students.

Jowett's funeral procession outside Balliol in 1893. As master of the college from 1870, he was a towering figure in Victorian Oxford and had once confessed to 'a general prejudice against all persons who do not succeed in the world'.

His technique for galvanizing the idle into action was blunt but apparently effective; Walter Morrison, for example, was summoned to his presence as Finals approached and told:

You are a fool. You must be sick of idling. It is too late for you to do much. But the class matters nothing. What does matter is the sense of power which comes from steady working.[3]

Another man remembered being sent for:

When he reported, the Master was writing, and merely paused to say: 'Sit down, Mr Barnes, you are working with Mr Donkin, are you not?' The culprit said he was, and sat down. Jowett wrote on, page after page, while the undergraduate fidgeted. Finally Jowett looked up and remarked: 'Mr Donkin says you are not. Good-morning.' After that the undergraduate was more inclined to work with Mr Donkin.[4]

First and foremost a Balliol man, Jowett is said to have told a friend: 'If we had a little more money, we could absorb the University.'[5] In 1882, however, he was elected vice-chancellor and initiated a wide range of schemes including a new laboratory, reform of the University Extension System and teaching in oriental languages.[6] He also ended the centuries-old ban on undergraduate drama, although actors in the first legitimate play, THE MERCHANT OF VENICE, still fell foul of the proctor and bulldogs in December 1883:

On the opening night, as we were coming from our temporary dressing-rooms – a bicycle shop next-door to the Town Hall – to gain the stage, an over-officious Proctor, instigated by a couple of surly bull-dogs, raided us. We not being in cap and gown, our names and addresses, in the usual way, were demanded. When it came to Bromley-Davenport's turn ('the Bromer', as we affectionately called him), he was so thoroughly imbued with the spirit of his part that he answered instantly – 'Launcelot Gobbo. Number 1, High Street, Venice.'[7]

In contrast to Jowett who viewed Oxford as a training ground for the service of the state, Mark Pattison, Rector of Lincoln from 1851 to 1884 saw the University's role as the promotion of learning. Tactless and sometimes very disagreeable – Charles Oman described him as 'a sort of troglodyte'[8] – Pattison still had a magnetic influence over his students and greatly stimulated the intellectual life of his college.[9] At the age of forty-nine he married the twenty-one-year-old Emelia Francis Strong and he was satirized as the pedantic Professor Forth in Rhoda Broughton's Oxford novel BELINDA:

'You have spelt *allegorical* with one *l*!' says the Professor, in a voice of resentful wonder.

'Have I?' she answers, bewildered and inattentive. 'And how many ought it to have?'

'A child of five years old would have been ashamed to perpetrate so gross a blunder!' resumes he, taking the sheet from before her, and indignantly holding it up for reprobation.

She heaves a heavy, furious sigh, and a sombre light comes into her great, gloomy eyes.[10]

William Spooner, Fellow of New College from 1867 and Warden from 1903, became so famous that his surname has given a word to the English language. A small, pink-faced albino, he always resembled a white-haired baby, and a rival for a New College scholarship in 1862 is said to have remarked: 'I do not mind who gets the scholarship, if that child *does not'.[11] The child did and, by the mid-1880s, he was known for Spoonerisms or, as he called them, 'occasional infelicities in verbal diction'.[12] The manufacture of Spoonerisms, most of them completely apocryphal, became a minor industry:*

Riding a bicycle: 'The well boiled icicle.'

To a delinquent undergraduate: 'You have tasted a whole worm. You have hissed my mystery lectures. You were fighting a liar in the quadrangle. You will leave by the town drain.'

A cat falling from a window: 'It popped on its little drawers.'

Giving out the hymn: 'Kinquering congs their titles take.'

A favourite winter sport: 'Scooting on his pate on the ice.'

A well-known Oxford custom: 'The whore's bed ceremony.'

To a lady at dinner: 'Pass the pig's fleas.'[13]

Among the many characterful dons, Charles Dodgson, or Lewis Carroll, achieved perhaps the most international reputation through his creation of ALICE IN WONDERLAND. Dodgson was made Student of Christ Church in 1852 and occupied the position of mathematical lecturer from 1855 to 1881. By taking their photographs and telling them fantastical stories, Dodgson gained the friendship of Dean Liddell's daughters, Alice, Lorina and Edith. Robinson Duckworth – 'Duck' in the book – later recalled the creation of ALICE IN WONDERLAND on 4 July 1862:

I rowed *stroke* and he rowed *bow* in the famous Long Vacation voyage to Godstow, when the three Miss Liddells were our passengers, and the story was actually composed and spoken *over my shoulder* for the benefit of Alice Liddell, who was acting as 'cox' of our gig. I remember turning round and saying, 'Dodgson, is this an extempore romance of yours?' And he replied, 'Yes, I'm inventing as we go along'. I also well remember how, when we had conducted the three children back to the Deanery, Alice said, as she bade us good-night, 'Oh, Mr Dodgson, I wish you would write out Alice's adventures for me'.[14]

A shy man who became almost a recluse in later years, Dodgson was described by Grundy as 'a somewhat silent, gloomy man'[15] and Ethel Hatch recalled his dislike of parties and 'bandying small talk with dull people'.[16] Nevertheless, a sense of humour was often present in his other writings, as, for example, when he described his three years as Curator of the Common Room at Christ Church:

Long and painful experience has taught me one great principle in managing business for other people, *viz*, if you want

William Archibald Spooner (1844–1930), the originator of the much-imitated Spoonerism. He entered New College as an undergraduate in 1862 and devoted the rest of his life to the college, being elected Fellow in 1867 and Warden in 1903.

A New College sermon: 'Which of us, my brothers, has not at some time cherished within his bosom a half-warmed fish?'

On April in town: 'Spring came with a funny sootfall, alternating tiles and smears, while occasionally she roared with pain under a mauling fist.'

The young mathematics lecturer, Charles Lutwidge Dodgson, better known as Lewis Carroll, in the late 1850s. Dodgson spent most of his life at Christ Church after matriculating there in 1850.

to inspire confidence, *give plenty of statistics*. It does not matter that they should be accurate, or even intelligible, so long as there is enough of them. A curator who contents himself with simply *doing* the business of a Common Room, and who puts out no statistics, is sure to be distrusted. 'He keeps us in the dark!' men will say. 'He publishes no figures. What does it mean? Is he assisting himself?' But, only circulate some abstruse tables of figures, particularly if printed in lines and columns, so that ordinary readers can make nothing of them, and all is changed at once. 'Oh, go on, go on!' they cry, satiated with facts. 'Manage things as you like! We trust you entirely.'[17]

John Ruskin, Slade Professor of Fine Art from 1869, was another towering figure. He set up a drawing school and art collection, hoping that

Any youths who have an eye for colour will, perhaps, by Heaven's help, sometimes find that there are rainbows elsewhere than in jockeys' jacket, before they get through their college life.[18]

Ruskin became disillusioned with lecturing and refused to lecture in Glasgow because

I find the desire of audiences to be audiences only becoming an actively pestilent character of the age. Everybody wants to hear – nobody to read, nobody to think; to be excited for an hour – and, if possible, amused; to get the knowledge it has cost a man half his life to gather, first sweetened up to make it palatable, and then kneaded into the smallest possible pills, and to swallow it homoeopathically and be wise – this is the passionate desire and hope of the multitude of the day.[19]

In Oxford, he saw the famous Hinksey road-digging experiment as a practical way of introducing his students to the concept of 'useful art'. In November 1873, he explained the scheme to Henry Acland:

John Ruskin (1819–1900), photographed by Sarah Angelina Acland in 1893. Ruskin was appointed Slade Professor of Fine Art in 1869 and later founded the Ruskin School of Drawing and Fine Art.

The North Hinksey road-menders in May 1874. John Ruskin's undergraduates learn the 'pleasures of useful muscular work' by trying to restore the road through the village.

Sir Henry Acland (1815–1900) with his pet monkey. Acland was Regius Professor of Medicine from 1857 to 1894 and a tireless campaigner for reform and improvement in Oxford.

My dear Acland,

In the first place, I want to show my Oxford drawing class, my notion of what a country road should be. I am always growling about rails, and I want them to see what I would have instead; beginning with quite a by-road through villages. Now I don't know in all England, a lovelier *site* of road, than the lane along the foot of the hills past Ferry Hinksey, and I want Dr Harcourt's leave to take up the bit of it, immediately to the south of the village, and bring it this spring into the prettiest shape I can. I want to level one or two bits where the water lodges; to get the ruts out of the rest, and sow the banks with the wild flowers that should grow on them; and this I want to do with delicate touching, putting no rough workmen on the ground, but keeping all loveliness it *has*. This is my first, not my chief object.

My chief object is to let my pupils feel the pleasure of *useful* muscular work, and especially of the various and amusing work, involved in getting a human pathway rightly made, through a lovely country, and rightly adorned . . .

I will send down my own gardener to be at their command, with what under work may here and there be necessary, which they cannot do with pleasure to themselves, and I will meet whatever expenses is needful for cartage and the like, . . .

I had more to say but my paper says, I suppose rightly, better not, except, I am

Ever your loving friend
John Ruskin[20]

The diggings attracted enormous attention and much derision, but at the end of 1874, Colonel Harcourt's surveyor reported that 'The young men have done no mischief to speak of'.[21] Ruskin's friend, Henry Acland, was Regius Professor of Medicine from 1857 to 1894 and 'profoundly interested in all that concerned the welfare of the human race, whether physically or morally'. In Oxford, he led the fight against the 1854 cholera epidemic, founded the Sarah Acland Home in memory of his wife, encouraged the development of the Radcliffe Infirmary and helped to set up the Cutler Boulter Provident

Dispensary. At one time he had an extensive medical practice and recalled being reprimanded by the doctor in attendance for prescribing some simple treatment:

When, Sir, we send for a physician from Oxford, we expect the prescription to come to at least a guinea. This comes to eighteen pence.

Acland was a crucial figure in the development of natural science at Oxford. When he became Lees Reader of Anatomy in 1846 practical demonstration was frowned upon and he had to keep his prize giraffe skeleton in an old Christ Church stable where the canons' dogs stole the tail bones. From 1847, he struggled to persuade the University to found a museum to illustrate and comprise the whole of physical science. Building began at last in June 1855 but the project was plagued by lack of funds and the University eventually decided not to spend a penny more on 'those useless decorations'.[22] The Irish stone carver O'Shea was dismissed and Acland recorded:

I found O'Shea on a single ladder in the porch wielding heavy blows such as one imagines the genius of Michael Angelo might have struck when he was first blocking out the design of some immortal work. 'What are you doing, O'Shea? I thought you were gone; and Mr Woodward has given no design for the long moulding in the hard green stone.' Striking on still, O'Shea shouted, 'Parrhots and Owwls! Parrhots and Owwls! Members of Convocation.' There they were blocked out alternately. What could I do? 'Well,' I said meditatively, 'O'Shea, you must knock their heads off'. 'Never,' says he. 'Directly,' say I.

Their heads went. Their bodies, not yet evolved, remain to testify to the humour, the force, the woes, the troubles in the character and art of our Irish brethren – much to love, much to direct, much to lament.[23]

The great geologist, William Buckland, surprisingly refused to support Acland's campaign for the museum, having concluded by

1847 that the cause of natural history in Oxford was 'utterly hopeless'. [24] Buckland was in fact a pioneer of science teaching at Oxford and his well-illustrated lectures were 'cheery, humorous, bustling, full of eloquence'. As this couplet recalls, geology was beginning to challenge long-accepted religious doctrines:

> Some doubts were once expressed about the Flood
> Buckland arose, and all was clear as – mud.

He was a quite extraordinary character who once caused a stir in a foreign cathedral by identifying so-called martyr's blood with his tongue as bats' urine. [25] In Oxford, he 'delighted the undergraduates of Ruskin's day by his intrepid attempt to eat his way through the animal kingdom. The toughest articles of his adventurous diet proved to be a blue-bottle and a mole.' [26] His appearance matched his behaviour:

I can see him now, passing rapidly through the quadrangle and down St. Aldate's – broad-brimmed hat, tailcoat, umbrella, great blue bag. Sir H. Davy once expected him, and disappointed, asked his servant if Dr Buckland had not called. 'No, sir, there has been no one but a man with a bag; he called three times, and I always told him you were out. [27]

The battle between science and religion reached a climax at the famous British Association meeting in 1860 which was held in the new University Museum. At the end of a paper about Darwin's views, the Bishop of Oxford, Samuel Wilberforce – nicknamed Soapy Sam – was encouraged to stand up and condemn the theory of evolution:

He ridiculed Darwin badly and Huxley savagely, but 'all in such dulcet tones', so persuasive a manner, and in such well-turned periods that all were delighted.

The Bishop spoke thus 'for full half-an-hour with inimitable spirit, emptiness, and unfairness'. 'In a light, scoffing tone, florid and fluent, he assured us there was nothing in the idea of evolution; rock-pigeons were what rock-pigeons had always been. Then, turning to his antagonist with a smiling insolence, he begged to know, was it through his grandfather or his grandmother that he claimed his descent from a monkey?'

This was the fatal mistake of his speech. Huxley instantly grasped the tactical advantage which the descent to personalities gave him. He turned to Sir Benjamin Brodie, who was sitting beside him, and emphatically striking his hand upon his knee, exclaimed, 'The Lord hath delivered him into mine hands'. The bearing of the exclamation did not dawn upon Sir Benjamin until after Huxley had completed his 'forcible and eloquent' answer to the scientific part of the Bishop's arguments, and proceeded to make his famous retort.

On this Mr Huxley slowly and deliberately arose. A slight, tall figure, stern and pale, very quiet and very grave, he stood before us and spoke those tremendous words – words which no one seems sure of now, nor, I think, could remember just after they were spoken, for their meaning took away our breath, though it left us in no doubt as to what it was. He was not ashamed to have a monkey for his ancestor; but he would be ashamed to be connected with a man who used great gifts to obscure the truth. No one doubted his meaning, and the effect was tremendous. One lady fainted and had to be carried out; I, for one, jumped out of my seat. [28]

After this, delegates anticipated more verbal fireworks:

'From the back of the platform emerged a clerical gentleman, asking for a blackboard. It was produced, and amid dead silence he chalked two crosses at its opposite corners, and stood pointing to them as if admiring his achievement. We gazed at him, and he at us, but nothing came of it, till suddenly the absurdity of the situation seemed to strike the whole assembly simultaneously. . . . Again and again the laughter pealed, as purposeless laughter is wont to do; under it the artist and his blackboard were gently persuaded to the rear, and we saw him no more. [29]

Charles Oman recalled an inaugural lecture which was only slightly longer than this clerical gentleman's fiasco. Frederick York Powell was an unconventional don who, according to Oman, 'spent his time in doing very pleasantly the things that he need not have done, and leaving undone the things which he ought to have done'. When he was made Regius Professor of Modern History in 1894 there were hopes that he would rise to the occasion:

Alas! the Regius Professorship made no alteration in his manner of life. His inaugural lecture, to which the whole university had thronged in hope of hearing something distinctive, was almost a scandal. He came in very late, and looking rather bored, with two or three scraps of paper in his hand. He made a few disjointed remarks for about twenty minutes, intimated that he had never known his predecessor Froude, so could not speak about him, and complained that Oxford was destitute of the proper apparatus for original research. When we were expecting him to warm up to some eloquent thesis, he suddenly slapped down the last of his scraps, observed that he had no more to say, and departed.[30]

At the other end of the scale, Cook Wilson, Professor of Logic, specialized in almost endless lectures. One evening, he and G.B. Grundy were to give short papers to a college society and Wilson began with a paper on 'The Undergirding of Ships'. Years later, Grundy still had vivid memories of the occasion:

Cook Wilson started off at 8.30 p.m. Up to 9.30 p.m he had not said a word about undergirding or even about ships. About that time I went to sleep. I was on a couch, with Macan next to me. I was awakened by what I dreamt was an earthquake; but it was Macan, who had also gone to sleep and had fallen against me. The time was then 10.30 p.m., and Cook Wilson was then saying, 'After these preliminary remarks . . . ' . I went over to the chairman of the meeting and whispered that I was going as it would be impossible for me to read my paper that evening. So I went out. Half the meeting followed me; and a very angry crowd they were.[31]

Cook Wilson had another quite different role as the 'skilful and fiery commander' of the University's bicycle corps. The cavalry despised the cyclists as inferior and unchivalrous but

it was not easy to despise Captain Wilson and his merry men, when one saw them drawn up in their most efficient formation for guarding a narrow way against the onset of cavalry, forty bicycles ranged close together with their saddles on the ground and their wheels whirring loud in the air and forty men lying behind them and firing through the spokes, with the grim vision of Wilson's beard looming through the smoke: an old cavalry-officer brought up to inspect swore and declared that no cavalry would face such an infernal machine.[32]

Many other dons etched their personalities and some of their mannerisms into the memories of others. Elizabeth Wordsworth remembered Walter Pater 'with his gentle, dreamy manner, his face all curves and no angles, his measured utterance (every word carefully chosen) and his genuine love for quaint and beautiful things'.[33] Dr John Bull of Christ Church was known for throwing open the windows 'to purify the atmosphere' after non-college men had attended his lectures.[34] R.W. Raper of Trinity College was memorable for his bizarre notices:

CRICKET MAY BE PLAYED BY MEMBERS OF THE
COLLEGE
ON THE LAWN IN THE COLLEGE GARDEN
on payment of a sum of one guinea by
each player on each occasion.

UNDERGRADUATE MEMBERS OF THE COLLEGE
WHO COME FROM FAMILIES WHERE THE
PRACTICE
OF THROWING BREAD OR OTHER EATABLES

PREVAILS AT MEALS MAY CONTINUE THE
PRACTICE IN THE COLLEGE HALL
on payment of a fine of half a guinea on the first
and larger sums on later occasions.[35]

*Sampson of Brasenose astounded colleagues by his intimate know-
ledge of BRADSHAW'S RAILWAY GUIDE and the Revd
Albert Watson — also of Brasenose — by his memory for racing
results.[36] The latter was also*

a proverb for his accuracy and excessive caution. My brother
John used to have a story against him *à propos* of an article in
some literary periodical. 'Watson, do you know who wrote
that article?' 'No, I don't. Anyhow, I didn't. But (with a sudden withdrawal of confidence) perhaps I ought not to have
said that.'[37]

*The Revd J.E. Sewell, Warden of New College, amused by ques-
tioning the need for new baths for undergraduates said: 'What do they
need baths for? They are only here for eight weeks at a time'.[38]
A.C. Clark, a Latin tutor of Queen's College, caused much mirth
when, with his cultivated stammer, he translated a passage: 'Phyllis,
let me — er — er kiss thy calves, — er — er thy heifers.'[39] Robinson Ellis,
Professor of Latin, was remarkable for his blissful ignorance of sexual
matters and an embarrassingly child-like curiosity:*

At a certain dinner-party he happened to sit next to a lady
who had recently produced twins, and to the intense
embarrassment of the company spent a large part of the
evening in cross-examining her on the respective merits of
producing families by ones or twos, and which method she
preferred.

Woods, the President of Trinity, married, and in due course
his wife produced her first child. Ellis, feeling he must
congratulate his old friend, wrote, 'My dear Woods, I must
congratulate you on the recent event which took me quite by
surprise. You no doubt were better informed.'[40]

*Professor Robinson Ellis (1834–1913), a caricature by the self-styled
Giovanni Casanova in 1902. Corpus Professor of Latin from 1893, Ellis
was perhaps the archetypal example of the unworldly Oxford don.*

By contrast, E.F. Carritt recalled 'another kind of ignorance which is attributed to all stage dons. An old gentleman, one of whose bicycle tyres was deflated, asked an undergraduate to pump it. The boy said,"Certainly; better tighten the other too". "Oh, thank you, but are they not connected?"'[41]

In their briefer Oxford careers and with their eccentricities perhaps less well developed, undergraduates rarely had as much chance as dons to leave a permanent mark on Oxford. Oscar Wilde was a major exception and within a year of matriculating at Magdalen College in 1874,

his picturesque panelled room overlooking the Cher had become the scene of regular Sunday evening gatherings, to which all his friends were welcome. On the table smoked two brimming bowls of gin-and-whisky punch; and long church-warden pipes, with a brand of choice tobacco, were provided for the guests. The meetings were gay and hilarious – not uproarious; and no one that I saw was ever the worse for the punch. There was generally music. And I remember my friend, Walter Parratt, the college organist, afterwards Master of the Queen's Musick at Windsor, whom we all liked, accompanying, with those marvellous fingers of his, Walter Smith-Dorrien's delightful rendering of some of the ballads of the day. Sometimes the general cheerfulness degenerated into a scuffle or romp, to the imminent danger of our host's bric-a-brac.[42]

Although Wilde tried to convey an impression of aesthetic indolence, he was in fact an assiduous scholar, winning the Newdigate Prize in 1877 and gaining a First. When asked his ambition, he replied:

God knows! I won't be a dried-up Oxford don, anyhow. I'll be a poet, a writer, a dramatist. Somehow or other I'll be famous, and if not famous, I'll be notorious.[43]

William Morris, at Exeter College from 1853 to 1855, also viewed dons as narrow-minded pedants and left Oxford with his

friend Edward Burne-Jones to embark upon 'a life of art'. While at Oxford, both men had become fascinated by the Pre-Raphaelites and they returned with Rossetti and others in the summer of 1857 to decorate the Oxford Union Debating Hall with frescoes of scenes from Malory's MORTE D'ARTHUR. The work progressed slowly in an atmosphere of uproar, practical jokes and much talk about 'stunners' or attractive young women. In 1859, Morris married a local 'stunner', Jane Burden, the daughter of an Oxford ostler, who had been asked to model by Rossetti and Burne-Jones after they spotted her at the theatre.[44]

Unlike Morris or Oscar Wilde, E.A. Freeman did go on to become a don and succeeded Bishop Stubbs as Regius Professor of Modern History in the 1880s. As an undergraduate, he was a man of very singular manners:

He paid no regard at all to what people might think of him, and he was in the habit of repeating poetry to himself as he walked in the streets, and occasionally leaping into the air when the poem moved him to any enthusiasm.[45]

His eccentricity was only refined by age and Ethel Hatch recalled the occasion when a friend found Professor Freeman in his hall

banging at the drawing-room door with his umbrella.
'Hullo, what's the matter?'
'Are any of the women about?' asked Freeman. 'I want a woman to roll up my umbrella; only a woman can roll up an umbrella'.
'They're all out', said the friend. 'Here, give me your umbrella and I'll roll it up'. The only thanks tendered were, 'Umph! You ought to have been a woman yourself!'[46]

Pet-keeping was a notable feature of the Victorian University and some pets achieved as much fame or notoriety as their masters. At William Buckland's rooms in Christ Church, Tuckwell recalled a profusion of animals:

The guinea-pig under the table inquiringly nibbled at your infantine toes, the bear walked round your chair and rasped your hand with file-like tongue, the jackal's fiendish yell close by came through the open window, the monkey's hairy arm extended itself suddenly over your shoulder to annex your fruit and walnuts.[47]

The bear was probably Tiglath Pileser which belonged to William's son Frank. Dressed in cap and gown, Tig

was taken to wine parties, or went boating with his master, to the wonderment of the children in Christ Church Meadow, who would follow them down the walk leading to the boats,

The bulldog Oriel Bill, wearing his boater, features proudly in the College photograph for 1895. He was virtually regarded as a member of Oriel College in the 1890s and it was claimed that he would only answer to an Oriel man.

regardless of expostulations and threats, until sometimes the bear was turned loose and shambled after them, whereupon they fled.

He also attended a British Association garden party at the Botanic Garden in 1847:

The bear sucked all our hands and was very caressing. Amid our shouts of laughter in the garden by moonlight, it was diverting to see two or three of the dons, who were very shy, not knowing how far their dignity was compromised.

Tig at last fell under the censure of the Dean of Christ Church. 'Mr Buckland', the Dean is reported to have said, 'I hear you keep a bear in the College; well, either you or your bear must go.'[48]

Less threatening perhaps than a bear, Oriel Bill was a brindled bulldog which, in the 1890s became almost an honorary member of Oriel College.

Never would he venture into college, save on the day in Summer Term when the college was photographed. Then he strode in, settled himself on a table in the midst of the group, and faced the camera with a placid courage. He knew every member of the college, and would go with an Oriel man anywhere, but to all others he turned a deaf ear. The most august member of the University valued his recognition, due to the fact that his name was on our books, and not the least distinguished of our Professors wrote on his appointment, 'my highest ambition is gratified, now that I am part owner of Oriel Bill'. His attendance at college matches, whether cricket or football, was unfailing, and thereby hangs a tale. He had been with the eleven to the Keble ground, the day was hot, and his energy exhausted by encouraging applause. Seeing a hansom just starting for the town, he jumped in and was driven home.[49]

Ice hockey in Christ Church Meadow in February 1895. The great freeze was ideal for this sport although the Torpids, for example, had to be cancelled.

CHAPTER FOUR

An Oxford Year

Of the hundreds of boys who are shot on the GWR platform every October to be caressed or kicked by Alma Mater, and returned in due time full or empty, it is only an insignificant minority who come up with the ostensible purpose of learning. Their reasons are as many as the colours of their portmanteaus. Brown has come up because he is in the sixth form at school, and was sent in for a scholarship by a head-master desiring an advertisement; Jones, because it is thought by his friends that he might get into the 'Varsity eleven; Robinson, because his father considers a University career to be a stepping-stone to the professions – which it fortunately is not as yet. Mr Sangazur is going to St. Boniface because his father was there; and Mr J. Sangazur Smith – well, probably because *his* father wasn't.[1]

During Victoria's reign the focus of attention at the beginning of each term shifted from the old coaching inns to the railway stations. When the fictional hero Verdant Green arrived at the 'Mitre' with his father in about 1850, 'they were attacked by a horde of the aborigines of Oxford who . . . swooped down upon them in the guise of impromptu porters, and made an indiscriminate attack upon their luggage.'[2] In 1890, Mrs Batty found an 'intricate maze of men and boxes, chests, banjos, tricycles, bicycles, fiddles, hatboxes and bags' on the Great Western Railway Station platform:

Two or three great luggage vans had already been emptied, their contents standing in groups and piles, sorted or oftener unsorted and unappropriated – and unexciting owners to claim them, or porters to remove them. Loafers had been pressed into the Service from outside, the little Smith's stall boys were exerting themselves to help superhumanly in the expectation of a copper here and there, but also in the superabundance of boyish energy. 'What College Sir?' enquires a porter as he wheels a barrow load of articles . . . amongst the feet of other parties, passengers and officials, saying, 'By your leave Sir, if you please' as he goes. St John's or New or Christ Church may be the response – and they issue through the railway portals – *en route* to a cab – the undergraduate with his fingers in his waistcoat pocket ready to fork out a tip.[3]

Reaching the college, the freshman was shown to his rooms. Verdant Green 'found his bedroom inconveniently small; so contracted, indeed, in its dimensions, that his toilette was not completed without his elbows having first suffered severe abrasions.'[4] In 1853, Augustus Hare wrote to his mother from No. 2, Kitchen Staircase at University College:

a room long and narrow, with yellow beams across the ceiling, and a tall window at one end admitting dingy light, with a view of straight gravel-walks, and beds of cabbages and rhubarb in the Master's kitchen garden. Here, for £32. 16s. 6d. I have been forced to become the owner of the last proprietor's furniture – curtains which drip with dirt, a bed with a ragged counterpane, a bleared mirror in a gilt frame, and some ugly mahogany chairs and tables. 'Your rooms might be worse, but your servant could not', said Mr Hedley when he brought me here.[5]

Some freshmen were considerably worse off than Hare. In 1899, the Revd W.K.R. Bedford recalled:

Even in such matters as ordinary sanitation and daily decency the arrangements in not a few of the best colleges were indescribably rude and filthy. . . . Even in so good a College as B.N.C., where the accommodation at the present day is somewhat limited, the overcrowding was such that occasionally a late comer was informed that he must submit to be billeted upon another man, whose set of rooms embraced two sleeping apartments. This, considerably to my disgust, I found was to be my fate when I entered Brasenose in the forties.[6]

Frederick Oakeley, entering Christ Church in 1820,

was bandied about from one set of rooms to another; and at length, to my great joy, sent home for want of a place where to lay my head. During those few weeks I conceived a disgust of college-life, which I never wholly conquered till after I took my degree. I found myself quite out of harmony with the society of the place. I would not go through for a trifle what I used to suffer in having to pass through a knot of buoyant undergraduates in Peckwater or at Canterbury Gate. My tutor kindly introduced me to two reading-men, who however, I suppose, were reading so hard that they did not want to be troubled with a new acquaintance, for both of them cut me the day after the introduction. I used to find relief in a good cry when I came to my unutterably dismal rooms in Fell's Buildings, after morning chapel or after hall, when I had seen clusters of my happier companions go off in high spirits to their several breakfast or wine-parties.[7]

The first dinner in hall was one of the fresher's biggest ordeals:

The senior men came up a day after us, and most freshers, until they settle down, seem to spend their time in waiting for somebody else to say something. The dinner really made me feel most gloomy; things seem to have been turned upside down, and in the process I felt as if I had fallen with a thud to the bottom. There were two or three freshers from Cliborough to whom I had scarcely spoken during my last two years at school, and these fellows all sat together and enjoyed themselves while I counted for nothing whatever. I began to learn the lesson that being in the Cliborough XI. and XV. was not a free passport to glory.[8]

That lesson duly learned, he could begin

to make acquaintances, over a newspaper in the junior common room, or at a preliminary visit to his tutor. With one, he walks up and down High Street: he learns which are the tailors and which are not. With another, he goes out to Parsons' Pleasure, and likes the willows of Mesopotamia, and sees New College Tower: he wants to loiter in the churchyard of Holy Cross, but is scornfully reminded that Byron did much the same. Queen's College inspires his companion with the remark that Queen in Oxford is called 'Quagger'. The Martyr's Memorial calls forth 'Maggers Memugger'; Worcester, 'Wuggins'; Jesus, 'Jaggers': and he is much derided when he supposes that the scouts use these terms.[9]

The undergraduate returning for his second or third year had the advantage of knowing, and being known by, everyone. For him, the first day of the Michaelmas Term was 'the brightest day of the year. . . .':

The Porter had acknowledged him at the gate, and the scout had smiled and bowed, as he ran up the worn staircase and found a blazing fire to welcome him. The coals crackled and split, and threw up a white flame in strong contrast with the newly-blackened bars and hobs of the grate. A shining copper kettle hissed and groaned under the internal torment of water at boiling point. The chimney-glass had been cleaned, the carpet beaten, the curtains fresh glazed. A tea-tray and tea-commons were placed on the table; besides a battel paper, two or three cards from tradesmen who desired his patronage, and a note from a friend whose term had already commenced. The porter came in with his luggage, and had just received his too ample remuneration, when through the closing doors, in rushed Sheffield in his travelling dress.

'Well, old fellow, how are you?' he said, shaking both of Charles's hands, or rather arms, with all his might, 'here we are all again; I am just come like you. Where have you been all this time? Come, tell us all about yourself. Give me some tea and let's have a good jolly chat.'[10]

By this time, too, the undergraduate would have had the opportunity to follow James Pycroft's advice in choosing a suitable room:

if the carpet is old you will always be covered with dust, so refuse the carpet, and order a new one. Look at the ceiling, and guess from the colour whether the fire smokes. Consider draughts, and see that the windows are in good order. Inquire whether it is a *rowing* or a quiet staircase. If a tutor's rooms are near, you will have a ready excuse for stopping all rough play and noise among your friends. A garret is too high to mount, and usually inconvenient. The ground-floor, or any rooms too much in the thoroughfare, are very objectionable, being the resort of loungers, while going to or from lecture. It is in vain to sport your oak when your friends can look through the window; for you will find that the frolicsome and light-hearted soon become too intimate to stand on ceremony. . . .

Lastly, consider whom you have overhead; for should he have the organ of music, and be always fiddling; the bump of pugnacity, and hold bread and cheese and porter meetings,

Fred Lyons, an undergraduate at Pembroke College, photographed in an Oxford studio in about 1860; his apparent seriousness is reinforced by the volume on the table and the studio backdrop of Oxford's towers and spires.

with boxing-gloves, single-stick, or some kinds of gymnastics, about luncheon-time every day; or, again, should he be one of the Peripatetic school, and be always pacing about his room; or declamatory, and given to spouting: in all these cases a neighbour may be very obnoxious, without being legally indictable for a nuisance.

Ryman's Eights Week print 'The Race', published in 1852. Crowds on the Oxfordshire bank watch from the shade of riverside willows as the crews race past Long Bridges. First recorded in 1815, the Eights became an annual event from 1824.

The Ashmolean Picture Gallery in about 1850. Fisher's drawing shows members of Oxford's social élite inspecting the pictures on the first floor of the Ashmolean Museum, a handsome Neo-Classical building by C.R. Cockerell which opened in 1845.

Still, when you have once chosen rooms, use every endeavour to live on good terms with all your neighbours. Never mind how different they may be from yourself in taste or character; there is some good to be found in most men. The wildest men are quietly disposed sometimes, just as many madmen have some lucid intervals; so, try to be on friendly terms, and to find a resource of some kind with all you meet, especially with those who live in the same staircase.[11]

One of Tom Brown's rich friends, Drysdale, had achieved a high degree of luxury at St Ambrose's College:

There were four deep windows, high up in the wall, with cushioned seats under them, two looking into the large quad-rangle, and two into the inner one. Outside these windows, Drysdale had rigged up hanging gardens, which were kept full of flowers by the first nurseryman in Oxford all the year round; so that even on this February morning, the scent of gardenia and violets pervaded the room, and strove for mastery with the smell of stale tobacco, which hung about the curtains and sofas. There was a large glass in an oak frame over the mantelpiece which was loaded with choice pipes and cigar-cases, and quaint receptacles for tobacco; and by the side of the glass hung small carved oak frames, containing lists of the meets of the Heythrop, the Old Berkshire, and Drake's hounds, for the current week. There was a queer assortment of well-framed paintings and engravings on the walls, several tandem and riding-whips, mounted in heavy silver, and a double-barrelled gun, and fishing-rods, occupied one corner, and a polished copper cask, holding about five gallons of mild ale, stood in another. In short, there was plenty of everything except books – the literature of the world being represented, so far as Tom could make out in his short scrutiny, by a few well-bound but badly used volumes of classics, with the cribs thereto appertaining, shoved away into a cupboard which stood half open, and contained besides, half-emptied

decanters, and large pewters, and dog-collars, and packs of cards, and all sorts of miscellaneous articles to serve as an antidote.[12]

The breakfast party was one of the pleasures of undergraduate life and Drysdale, together with three others in the fast set, established a breakfast club in which

real scientific gastronomy was cultivated. Every morning the boy from the Weirs arrived with freshly-caught gudgeon, and now and then an eel or trout, which the scouts on the staircase had learnt to fry delicately in oil. Fresh watercresses came in the same basket, and the college kitchen furnished a spitchcocked chicken, or grilled turkey's leg. In the season there were plover's eggs; or at the worst, there was a dainty omelette; and a distant baker, famed for his light rolls and high charges, sent in the bread – the common domestic col-lege loaf being of course out of the question for any one with the slightest pretensions to taste, and fit only for the perquisite of scouts. Then there would be a deep Yorkshire pie, or reservoir of potted game, as a *pièce de résistance*, and three or four sorts of preserves; and a large cool tankard of cider or ale cup to finish up with, or soda-water and maraschino for a change.[13]

Exercise was certainly needed after a meal like this but, in the 1830s comparatively few recreations were available to undergraduates:

At that time there was no football and no 'sports'; only one cricket field, the 'Magdalen ground', at the Oxford end of Cowley marsh. Comparatively few men boated; outriggers, dingies, canoes, apolaustic punts were unknown. Rich men hunted, followed the drag, jumped horses over hurdles on Bullingdon Green, drove tandem. . .[14]

Hunting was extremely popular at a time when many undergradu-ates were the sons of country gentlemen:

In olden days there were no lectures at the 'House' on Saints' days, which were therefore free for hunting. Unfortunately, chapels were absolutely compulsory, nor were the gates of the college opened until the service was over. Men therefore got into the habit of putting on their 'pink' before going to Chapel, where it was hidden by the surplice which all wore.[15]

So spectacular was the hunting that, in 1851, Samuel Sidney recommended visitors to:

take the ugliest road out of Oxford, by the seven bridges, because there you may see farthest along the straight highway from the crown of the bridges, and number the ingenuous youth as on hunters they pace, or in hack or in dogcart or tandem they dash along to the 'Meet'. Arrived there, if the fox does get away – if no ambitious youngster heads him back – if no steeplechasing lot ride over the scent and before the hounds, to the destruction of sport and the *master's* temper – why then you will see a fiery charge at fences that will do your heart good. There is not such raw material for cavalry in any other city in Europe, and there is no part of our social life so entirely novel, and so well worth exhibiting to a foreigner, as a 'Meet' near Oxford, where in scarlet and in black, in hats and in velvet caps, in top-boots and black-jacks, on twenty pound hacks and two hundred guinea hunters, finest specimens of Young England are to be seen.
On returning, if the sport has been good, you may venture to open a chat with a well-splashed fellow traveller on a beaten horse, but in going not – for an Oxford man in his normal state never speaks unless he has been introduced.[16]

Football and athletics began to gain ground as autumn sports in the 1850s although the Revd G.V. Cox was aggrieved at 'the absurd exhibition . . . of men (and gentlemen) jumping (or attempting to jump) in sacks sewed up to the shoulders, forty yards out and forty yards in, round a flag!'.[17] The first University Athletics Meeting was held at the

Magdalen Ground on Cowley Marsh in December 1860 in the presence of Edward, Prince of Wales. Despite the mud and rain,

his happy-looking countenance was to be seen in all parts of the field, mixing with his brother undergraduates, in the most kind and affable manner. His demeanour also towards the citizens, while smoking his cigar under the pavilion, was just what Englishmen would expect from the son of our beloved Queen.[18]

In athletics, as in other sports, Oxford gloried in its amateurism, to the evident incredulity of the American John Corbin. He was surprised that nobody sought out athletes among the freshmen and that Oxford had no professional trainer:

The nearest approach to it was the groundsman at the Iffley Running Grounds, a retired professional who stoked the boilers for the baths, rolled the cinder-path, and occasionally acted as 'starter'. As his 'professional' reputation as a trainer was not at stake in the fortunes of the Oxford team, his attitude was humbly advisory. The president of the Athletic Club never came near the grounds, being busy with rowing on a 'varsity trial eight, and later with playing Association football for the University.[19]

As winter set in, many took to indoor amusements. A.M.M. Stedman suggested that undergraduates spend the hour before 6 o'clock dinner 'in reading at the Union or the Clubs, in shopping, at that new institution, afternoon tea or at billiards'. He warned against shopping as being potentially expensive but defended billiards against its detractors as 'a particularly fascinating game'. The Oxford Union, founded as a debating club in 1823, afforded every opportunity

to those desirous of improving their minds. Apart from the debates, which are naturally a very important feature, every facility is afforded for universal reading. There are six or seven

paper, envelopes, etc., are supplied, and letters gratuitously stamped. It is a natural result that this room should be generally crowded by undergraduates, whose eager desire is to equal their subscription by the value of stamps consumed . . .[20]

For Margaret Jeune, wife of the Master of Pembroke, winter evenings brought a busy round of social engagements:

1854, 3rd November. Thursday.

On looking over my visiting book we find we must give another dinner this term. Also we have made the discovery that in the case of the Blisses and Coopers, it is *we* not *they* who have appeared to drop the acquaintance by not inviting them in turn, and now it is too late to mend the matter. Mrs Bliss I know is extremely punctilious as to returning *dinner for dinner*, so I suppose we may consider them quite struck off our visiting list. The loss is certainly not great!

1858, 27th October. Wednesday.

Dined at Wadham – a grand party and in the evening a somewhat alarming incident occurred to enliven the evening. Mrs S. was handing about a beautiful specimen of the New Zealand grass – it was 6 feet in height in the stalk and a beautiful feather waved at the top. She was replacing it in the corner, when, the tip bending over a candle, caught fire, in a moment the whole room was in a blaze of light. Lady Anstruther shrieked awfully, and it appeared inevitable that not only Mrs S. but all the other lace and muslin in the room should be in flames, but she rushed to the fire, and Mr Warren, who was playing on the piano, jumped up, and dashed it from her hand into the fire. It was a narrow escape for us all, and I am sure we must have felt it was a merciful preservation.

On 31 December 1855 she had the unusual experience of celebrating the New Year an hour early:

Verdant Green, expensively tutored by Mr Fluke of Christ Church, learns to play billiards, one of Victorian Oxford's favourite indoor games.

large rooms apportioned to different branches of literature, ephemeral or otherwise. In one room are the daily papers, in another the weekly periodicals, in another the various magazines. There is a large library where every work likely to assist the studies, or amuse the leisure hours of students, may be found, unless dishonest members have appropriated these volumes to their own use. There is, too, a writing-room, where

The beginning of the Torpids in February 1888. Despite the cold and snow, undaunted oarsmen wait eagerly for the starting-gun and the chance to get warm.

A tea-party in the garden for the young ladies of Somerville Hall in 1895.

I took the children at 7 to Mr Hozier's rooms at Balliol and a very pleasant evening we had. Dancing, a Magic Lantern and a Christmas Tree were the amusements of the evening, and the principal object of the party being 'to see the New Year in', and the Master of Balliol not choosing to permit anyone remaining in College after 12, the difficulty was met by advancing the Clock an hour, so just before the imaginary closing of the old worn-out year, our host went round with the Grace-cup, offering each guest to 'drink to the Year that's awa'. This duty performed 'Auld Lang Syne' was sung, the guests holding each other with crossed hands. To fill up the time till the clock struck, 'He's a jolly good fellow' was jollily led by Mrs Liddell, and immediately the would-be hour of midnight sounded, our host went round again, bidding us drink 'a happy New Year to the Company', and the ceremony was loyally concluded by 'God save the Queen' – Mr Hozier being a Scotchman was the occasion of its being performed in this, the fashion of his country. We were at home by 11¹/₂ and I had the pleasure of giving a kiss to my dear husband as the New Year *really* broke on us – [21]

During the Victorian period, the Lent Term became noted for the Torpids, races for College Eights that were first rowed in winter in 1852.

The success of this improbable fixture – often rowed in appalling conditions – was part of the contemporary explosion of interest in rowing. At Oxford, the sport was greatly boosted in 1843 when a seven-man crew beat Cambridge in the Boat Race after the latter had refused to allow a last-minute substitution because of illness.[22]

Rowing was seen not only as a noble exercise but also as a way of bringing honour to the oarsman's college. Stedman saw participation as 'almost a necessary element in a University education' although he recognized the draw-backs:

Certainly boating as practised at Oxford is not an unmixed pleasure, and the necessity of sitting quietly in deshabille beneath a steady rain or fall of snow tends naturally to diminish the enthusiasm of a novice. Moreover, the operation which most must submit to, and which is technically termed 'coaching', involves the duty of bearing patiently the lusty and liberal abuse which the 'coach' often pours forth upon the unfortunate freshman, whose active anxiety to satisfy his stern monitor is generally rewarded by a concussion with his oar, and the undignified backward motion which is called 'catching a crab'.[23]

Even for those who preferred to stay indoors, a degree of heroism was still necessary. On 13 February 1895, H.W.B. Joseph, Fellow of New College recorded:

For the first time for many days there was no ice in my bath this morning: but 23° of frost were registered in Oxford during the night.[24]

The ever wondering American, John Corbin, went to his first dinner with the dons of his college and

the company assembled about a huge sea-coal fire. On a rough calculation the coal it consumed, if used in one of our steam-heaters, would have heated the entire college to incandescence. As it was, its only effect seemed to be to draw an icy blast across our ankles from medieval doors and windows that swept the fire bodily up the chimney, and left us shivering. One of the dons explained that an open fire has two supreme advantages: it is the most cheerful thing in life, and it insures thorough ventilation. I agreed with him heartily, warming one ankle in my palms, but demurred that in an American winter heat was as necessary as cheerfulness and ventilation.

'But if one wears thick woolens,' he replied, 'the cold and draught are quite endurable. When you get too cold reading, put on your great-coat.' I asked him what he did when he went out of doors. ' I take off my great-coat. It is much warmer there, especially if one walks briskly.'[25]

The University College 'B' team prepares to leave by coach and four for a cricket match at Wallingford in 1908.

At Brasenose College, the fancy-dress ball provided another way of keeping warm,

all the guests being of the sterner sex, but sundry ludicrous assumptions of female attire furnishing a semblance of the other element in ordinary reunions. . .; the stroke oar of our boat, a hirsute giant, had assumed the garb of a Red Indian, and made himself so intolerable, as the violence of his exertions in the war-dance caused the paint with which he was plentifully besmeared to dissolve, that he had been forcibly requested to retire to his wigwam.[26]

After Easter, the undergraduates re-assembled for the Summer Term:

the most pleasant of all terms – perhaps, indeed, the most enjoyable epoch of a lifetime. During the greater portion of it there are perpetual opportunities for amusement. Rowing, cricket, lawn-tennis, croquet, archery, garden-parties, flower-shows, should furnish interest to the most languid. What can be more charming than to float lazily down the Cherwell, shaded from the sun by the overspreading trees, or listlessly to saunter beneath elms and beeches in the fine old gardens? If more active amusements are sought, one may run with the eight along the river path, or pull down to Sandford, to fish, or bathe in the 'lasher'.[27]

It was a perfect time for the undergraduate like C.F. Cholmondeley of New College who played or watched sport, bathed at Parsons' Pleasure, or cycled off to Woodstock on a social tricycle with his friend Gee. As his diary entry for 20 April 1885 indicates, it was necessary – probably for financial reasons – to keep up appearances:

Fine day, I went up to our cricket ground and had some cricket practice, but did not get any of the professional's bowling. I went to be photographed by Hills and Saunders in a studious position to make Papa think I work.[28]

Picnickers at Iffley Lock on their way to Nuneham in 1882. Nuneham Park was a favourite destination, offering refreshments at the Lock Cottages and a choice of picnic places in romantic woodland or riverside settings.

Corbin found slackers aplenty on the River Cherwell:

The slackers you see tied up on the bank on both sides of the Char are always here after luncheon. An hour later their craft will be as thick as money-bugs on the water, and the joys of the slackers will be at height. You won't, as a rule, detect happiness in their faces, but it is always obvious in the name of the craft. One man calls his canoe *Vix Satis* which is the mark the university examining board uses to signify that a man's examination paper is a failure. Another has *P.T.O.* on his bows – the 'Please Turn Over' which an Englishman places at the bottom of a card where we say 'Over'. Still another calls his canoe the *Non-conformist Conscience* – which, as you are expected to remark, is very easily upset. All this makes the slacker even happier than if he were so un-English as to smile his pleasure, for he has a joke ready-made on his bow, where there is no risk of anyone's not seeing it.[29]

Cricket provided a welcome distraction for many undergraduates and, at the highest level the Varsity XI beat the touring Australians in 1884.[30] The author of this SOLILOQUY OF A BATSMAN probably had lower aspirations:

To slog or not to slog: that is the question:
Whether 'tis better every ball to smite,
Of pitch and pace regardless: or to cut:
To pull a leg: to drive: to block: to poke,
When on the wicket dead – To slog: to miss:
No more: and by that miss to end
My brief but pleasant life before the 'sticks'
My 'duck' unbroken and my wicket down
To some deceitful ball. – To slog: to hit
To hit: perchance to score: ay, there's the rub:
To break the cipher by some flukey runs,
While sweating fieldsmen tear across the mead
To catch the scudding ball. But now no more!
The bowler takes his stand to 'gin the attack
On my uncovered stumps. Ye gods, assist,
And guide the seasoned willow that I wield
Against the hostile ball, that all too straight
Approaches. Shall I smite with all my strength
And chance some lucky stroke? Methinks I will.[31]

On the river, Eights Week became the premier sporting event of the term and part of the social calendar. In the Oxford novel, the hero inevitably became the Saviour of the College Eight:

'START!'
The word sounded clear from the mouth of the 'Varsity captain of boats, and at once Ralph exerted the full force of Herculean arms. His blade struck the water a full second before any other; the lad had started well. Nor did he flag as the race wore on: as the others tired, he seemed to grow more fresh, until at length, as the boats began to near the winning-post, his oar was dipping into the water nearly twice as often as any other. . . .

And now the climax of the race was reached, and Ralph put forth his full strength; his oar clashed against those of 'Six' and 'Eight', the water foamed where his rowlock kept striking it, the boat shot forward, and slowly left St. Catherine's behind. *Ralph had saved the race!*[32]

There was intense excitement on the bank as each crew struggled to become Head of the River:

The noise of rattles, bells, pistols, whistles, bagpipes, frying-pans, and shouts can be heard in all the colleges and in the fields at Marston and Hinksey, where it has a kind of melody. Close at hand, it has a charm for the experienced tympanum: for in the cries of the victorious colleges the joy of victory is too great to allow of any discordant crow of mere triumph; the cries of those about to be beaten are too determined to have in them anything of hate. Such is the devout enthusiasm of the runners on the bank that if their own college boat is bumped they will sometimes run on to cheer the next boat that passes. The mysteries of harmony are never so wonderful as when, opposite the barge of a college that has made its bump, the sound of a hundred voices and a hundred instruments goes up, from dons, clergymen, old members of the college, future bishops, governors, brewers, schoolmasters, literary men, all looking very much the same, and in their pride of college forgetting all other pride.[33]

For the winners lively celebrations ensued and on 25 May 1887 Cholmondeley reported:

Tonight our eight left Magdalen far behind and were thus head of the river for the first time since the college was founded. We had a rather uproarious dinner in hall and afterwards had a display of fireworks by Brock and a big bonfire. A lot of Brasenose men came in amongst others and made their presence very noticeable. We went to the Warden's house after dinner and called on him to make a speech which he did.[34]

The crowd on the New College Barge watches the College Eight set off for the start during Eights Week in the 1900s.

Examinations cast a depressing shadow over early June for those who could no longer avoid them. After that, Commemoration or Commem Week formed the social climax of the Oxford year, most notable perhaps in an overwhelmingly male society for the sudden influx of young women, particularly the sisters and cousins of undergraduates. On Sunday, after the University Sermon in St Mary's church, the Show Sunday promenade in Christ Church Meadow attracted both Town and Gown,

and citizens of all ranks, the poorer ones accompanied by children of all ages, trooped along cheek by jowl with members of the University, of all degrees, and their visitors, somewhat indeed to the disgust of certain of these latter, many of whom declared that the whole thing was spoilt by the miscellaneousness of the crowd, and that 'those sort of people' ought not to be allowed to come to the Long Walk on Show Sunday. However, 'those sort of people' abounded nevertheless, and seemed to enjoy very much, in sober fashion, the solemn march up and down beneath the grand avenue of elms in the midst of their betters.[35]

The week continued with fashionable concerts and a flower show and college balls such as the one at St John's which Catherine Lucy attended on 17 June 1891:

At 9 we started for the Buttery Ball, St Johns. Mr Maxse got me a programme and introduced me to Mr Cheeke, who also put his name down. Mr Maxse followed us in and introduced me to Mr Greenland, then Stennett appeared and introduced Mr Simpson who introduced me to Mr Ashworth. Stennett introduced Mr Sanderson and Mr Maxse to Mr Arbuthnot and Edith intro. Mr Wilson. . . .

During the 10th dance, Mr Wilson gave me a steward's rosette which during the interval following Mr Maxse claimed as his and took despite my remonstrances. But the special thing of the evening was when Mr Maxse took me to his rooms, which are perfectly charming, they are hung with rather dark claret-coloured brocaded silk which looks like a paper and against which the pictures, statuette, vases etc., stand out well. He had the room crowded with plants and lighted with a pink lamp with a wonderful shade. He put me into the most comfortable chair with about 6 cushions, squirted scent over me and gave me grapes and then: played to me, he plays divinely. While he was playing Edith came in with Mr Wilson. Soon after that it struck two and we were obliged to stop, we finished up with 'Auld Lang Syne'.[36]

The rowdiest event of the week was the Encaenia Ceremony where honorary degrees were awarded at the Sheldonian Theatre. In 1843, the proceedings had to be abandoned when undergraduates roared their disapproval of Mr Jelf, a fiercely disciplinarian Junior Proctor.[37] More typical were the scenes in 1871 when

a gowned gentleman put in an appearance with a gorgeous neck tie of the hue of the common peony. Instantly there arose the shout of 'Red tie' accompanied with groans and hisses and cries of 'Go out, Sir'. After a while the cry became rhythmical, and accompanied by regular stamping, as though a monster fire-engine was being worked with a will. This was kept up for five minutes at a time, but 'Red tie' braved this and the stare of all present; he would neither go out nor give in. In the interval he was asked whether he hadn't got another tie, and was otherwise chaffed. To one of the 'gods' presently occurred a generous method of getting him out of the difficulty, and a white tie was thrown down to him. He had not, however, the ready wit to cover himself with distinction and win the favour of those who were as irate with the obnoxious colour as ever was a bull with a red flag, by donning the gift which somebody picked up and offered to him; and so the fire-engine was again in full operation and continued so with slight intermission for more than half-an-hour. . . .[38]

After this glorious confection of fashionable events and end-of-term mayhem, the year was over and

Show Sunday in Christ Church Meadow in about 1870. This opening event of Commemoration Week was an occasion to see and to be seen although the famous and fashionable rubbed shoulders with curious townsfolk and their families.

Watched by Town and Gown, the Encaenia procession leaves Queen's College for the Sheldonian Theatre in June 1897. The honorary graduates in that year included Horace Hart and Henry Frowde, two key figures in the late Victorian development of the University Press.

Uproar in the Undergraduates' Gallery at the Sheldonian Theatre before the Encaenia Ceremony in 1870. Rowdy behaviour, usually directed at inappropriately dressed visitors, helped to pass the time until the Chancellor's procession arrived.

Oxford was in a bustle of departure. The play had been played, the long vacation had begun, and visitors and members seemed equally anxious to be off. At the gates of the colleges groups of men in travelling dresses waited for the coaches, omnibuses, dog-carts, and all manner of vehicles, which were to carry them to the Great Western railway station at Steventon, or elsewhere, to all points of the compass. Porters passed in and out with portmanteaus, gun-cases, and baggage of all kinds, which they piled outside the gates, or carried off to 'The Mitre' or 'The Angel' under the vigorous and not too courteous orders of the owners. College servants flitted round the groups to take last instructions, and, if so might be, to extract the balances of extortionate bills out of their departing masters. Dog-fanciers were there also, holding terriers; and scouts from the cricketing grounds, with bats and pads under their arms; and ostlers, and men from the boats, all on the same errand of getting the last shilling out of their patrons – a fawning, obsequious crowd for the most part, with here and there a sturdy Briton who felt that he was only there for his due.[39]

Five members of the Alpine Club attain the summit on the south face of High Street in 1906. Charles Oman, proctor in the mid-1890s, recalled several encounters with intrepid climbers who needed to be shown the error of their ways.

CHAPTER FIVE

Undergraduate Discipline

I

If a Proctor meet a body
Coming down the High,
If a Proctor greet a body
Need a body fly?

II

Every Proctor has his bulldog
Dog of mickle might
When he marches forth in full tog
At the fall of night.

III

Every bulldog when he spies a
Man without a gown
Promptly chases him and tries a –
Main to run him down. [1]

The proctors were the terror of errant undergraduates, being charged to preserve order and keep Oxford free from improper characters. They were appointed from each college in rotation and nominated four pro-proctors to assist them. When they went out on their evening patrols they were accompanied by the University Marshal, their non-commissioned officer, and two or three of the 'bulldogs', as undergraduates called them. Charles Oman recalled these patrols at the end of the nineteenth century:

The Marshal was a most intelligent person, for long years a sergeant in the Oxfordshire Light Infantry, and very much the old soldier. I had many an amusing conversation with him, when business was slack and streets empty during our nocturnal rambles. The bulldogs were all middle-aged or elderly men, not chosen for their powers of running, but for their encyclopaedic knowledge of undergraduate personalities. Within a few weeks of the beginning of the Academic year they had usually obtained a very fair idea as to which of the freshmen were sly or noisy boys, while among the second and third year men they had a marvellous acquaintance with our usually very genial and amusing 'criminal classes'. The Marshal and the senior bull-dog had both of them extraordinary capacities of long sight: while we were fifty yards away they would warn me 'members of the A club going home in liquor', or

A run with the Ἀνθρωπο Θηρώμενοι Hounds.

Drawing the Covert

Full Cry

Gone Away

At Fault.

The Finish

The Brush

A run with the hounds in the early 1900s. An artist's impression of an undergraduate being chased and apprehended by the bulldogs and facing the proctor in the cold light of the next morning.

'Mr B. of C. College clinging to a post', or 'Mr D. going along breaking gas-lamps again', or occasionally 'a member and a "character" down that dark entry'. If a fleet-footed suspect absconded, he was not generally followed, for the chances were that he was known by sight to one of the proctorial band; if not, he could certainly have outrun a pursuer of forty-five years of age. The individuals with whom I had to deal were generally *not* in a condition to use their heels to any great effect. The bulldogs, besides their wonderful acquaintance with the junior academic public had also a sight-knowledge of certain undesirable town-dwellers of both sexes, 'bookies', 'touts', and light ladies who occasionally came under our notice.[2]

The struggle against 'light ladies' had been the major reason for the establishment of the University police in 1829 and even after the city established its own day police force in 1836 the University retained the night-watch. The report books of the force reveal the high level of surveillance that was exercised:

1856 April 25th & 26th Friday Night. . . .

No. 12 brought to the Rooms at Eleven o' Clock a Common Woman named Ann Walker who was found in company with a Member of the University at the back of St. John's Street – detained – He likewise with the Sub-Inspector brought to the Rooms at ten minutes before Twelve another Common Woman named Matilda Lewis who was found in Magdalen Street insulting two Gentlemen as they were passing quietly along the Street – detained – The Sub-Inspector and 7 also brought to the Rooms at ½ past Twelve another Common Woman named Eliza Fathers who was found talking to a Member of the University in St Aldates – detained – the Gentleman was followed to Christ Church at a ¼ past Twelve and the Porter told to notice him.[3]

In 1869, the separate University and city police forces were merged, but the proctors and bulldogs continued their efforts to enforce moral restraint. A rueful 'Member of the University' complained:

It does seem strange that, while the Proctors and their 'bulldogs' are so hard upon young girls of attractive appearance, old stagers and hardened offenders are nightly allowed to frequent regular haunts and to flaunt their vice in the faces of all sorts

THE CHAR-PROG.

The Char-Prog, a nightmare vision of a waterborne proctor and bulldogs surprising an undergraduate and his girlfriend in a punt.

of passers-by. Presumably their charms are not considered sufficiently seductive for undergraduate taste, and they are left to work their havoc upon the less epicurean citizen.[4]

Unceasing vigilance certainly had its successes and, in 1892, information from a college servant who lived nearby led to the discovery of a brothel in Kingston Road:

William Harvey, Proctor's servant, of 7, Canal Street, deposed that on the 27th of November . . . he saw a gentleman leave the house.

Mrs Brown – Yes, it was my daughter's sweetheart. (Laughter)

Harvey, continuing, said the man on leaving went to Keble College. On December 1 he saw a member of the University enter the house, and he fetched the Senior Proctor. He told Mrs Brown that the Senior Proctor had every reason to believe there was a member of the University there. She said it was a mistake, and there was no one there. Mr Brown said he had only just come in, and knew nothing about it. They went

upstairs and found a member of the University in the front bedroom with a young girl of about 18. They went into the bedroom and found them there undressed.[5]

In the economic circumstances of Victorian Oxford, however, it was virtually impossible to conquer prostitution and 'A Poor Law Guardian' complained in November 1874 that he had passed eight prostitutes in Cornmarket Street on a Tuesday afternoon; on Monday at about 10 p.m. he had passed thirteen between St Michael's Street and Carfax 'and that on one side of the street only'.[6] 'A Young Citizen' echoed his complaint, remarking that he was 'now no longer bidden a civil good-night, or nudged in passing, but stopped, followed, or solicited in the plainest terms.'[7]

The fictional Tom Brown was able to flirt with Patty, barmaid of The Choughs without hindrance:

Tom went out with the last batch of them, but lingered a moment in the passage outside. He knew the house and its ways well enough by this time. The next moment Patty appeared from a side door, which led to another part of the house.

'So you're not going to stay and play a game with aunt', she said; 'what makes you in such a hurry?'

'I must go up to college; there's a supper to celebrate our getting head of the river.' Patty looked down and pouted a little. Tom took her hand, and said sentimentally, 'Don't be cross, now; you know that I would sooner stay here, don't you? . . .'

'You shan't go, however, till you've given me that handkerchief. You promised it me if you got head of the river.'

'Oh! you little story-teller. Why they are my college colours. I wouldn't part with them for worlds. I'll give you a lock of my hair, and the prettiest handkerchief you can find in Oxford; but not this.'

'But I *will* have it, and you *did* promise me it' she said, and put up her hands suddenly, and untied the bow of Tom's neck-handkerchief. He caught her wrists in his hands, and looked down into her eyes in which, if he saw a little pique at

Christ Church and St Aldate's depicted by Shuffrey in 1906. Town houses on the left contrast with the magnigicent sixteenth-century front of Christ Church, completed by Sir Christopher Wren's Tom Tower in 1681–2. Tramlines, laid down in 1887, had been a minor Victorian addition to this scene.

The village of Iffley near Oxford, a drawing by Peter De Wint before 1834. River traffic was still flourishing, although bargees had sometimes to run the gauntlet of Varsity oarsmen. Within a decade, the coming of the railways was to decimate trade on the Thames.

his going, he saw other things which stirred in him strange feelings of triumph and tenderness.

'Well, then, you shall pay for it, anyhow,' he said. – Why need I tell what followed? – There was a little struggle; a 'Go along do, Mr Brown'; and the next minute Tom, minus his handkerchief, was hurrying after his companions; and Patty was watching him from the door, and setting her cap to rights.'[8]

Mark Tellar evaded proctoral patrols to walk shop-girls into remote corners of the city:

In my second year I made the acquaintance, by speaking to her in the street, of a girl who was an assistant in a large drapery shop. We went for walks in the evening; generally in Port Meadow, or near Jacob's Ladder. . . . She was a good-looking, quiet, virtuous girl. A kiss was the limit of the familiarities she allowed. Our association did not last long. She was succeeded by a second shop-girl: Clara Brinton. Her father kept a greengrocery and flower shop where I used to buy fruit. She was of a different type from the other girl: robust, athletic, high-spirited, tomboyish. I called her 'my Amazon'.[9]

T.E. Brown's poem MAGDALEN WALK recalls another Town and Gown relationship:

Ah little mill, you're rumbling still,
Ah sunset flecked with gold!
Ah deepening tinge, ah purple fringe
Of lilac as of old.
Ah hawthorn hedge, ah light-worn pledge
Of kisses warm and plenty,
When she was true and twenty-two,
And I was two-and-twenty.
I don't know how she broke her vow –
She said that I was 'horty';
And there's the mill a-goin' still,
And I am five-and-forty.

And sooth to tell, 'twas just as well
Her aitches were uncertain;
Her ways though nice, not point-device;
Her father liked his 'Burton'.
But there's a place you cannot trace,
So spare the fond endeavour –
A cloudless sky, where Kate and I
Are twenty-two for ever.[10]

Undergraduates might also try to socialize outside Oxford, although one such dance at Eaton near Appleton was interrupted and the house surrounded:

A cry arose – 'the Proctors! the Proctors!' – and all was in confusion. The Proctors entered and searched the room, knowing that six undergraduates were implicated, but could only find five. They took the names of these, and after an ineffectual search left the house. A few days after an undergraduate was visited by the Marshall, who informed him that the Proctor wished to see him. On reaching the Proctor's presence he was thus addressed – 'I am sure, sir, you would not tell a falsehood, and I will not tempt you to do it; so I will tell you what has come to my knowledge. You were at the ball given a few nights ago at Eaton. We searched the house but could not find you, though we discovered your five companions; you escaped in this way. When the confusion began, you threw yourself on your hands and knees on the floor; three of the female dancers sat upon your back, and spreading out their dresses effectually concealed you. You must be aware that you were guilty of a serious breach of discipline, but you have made no remark on my statement, and the mode of escape was so ingenious that I am reluctant to punish you, and therefore wish you good morning.'[11]

The University resisted the coming of the railway to Oxford as a potential threat to undergraduate discipline and the Oxford Railway Act of 1843 contained clauses which duly preserved proctoral authority:

CCCIV. And be it enacted, That the Vice Chancellor, the Proctors, and Pro-proctors for the Time being of the University of *Oxford*, and Heads of Colleges and Halls, and the Marshal of the said University, or other Person or Persons (provided such other Person or Persons shall have been deputed by Writing under the Hand of the Vice Chancellor of the said University for the Time being, or of the head or Governor, or, in his Absence, the Vicegerent of any College or Hall in the said University), shall, at or about the Times of Trains of Carriages upon the said Railway starting or arriving, and at all other reasonable Times, have free Access to every Depot or Station for the Reception of Passengers upon the said Railway, wheresoever such Office or Place shall be, and shall then and there be entitled to demand and take and have, without any unreasonable Delay, from the proper Officer or Servant of the Company, such Information as it may be in the power of any Officer or Servant of the Company to give, with reference to any Passenger or Person having passed or applying to pass on the said Railway, or otherwise coming to or being in or upon the said Depot or Station of Place, who shall be a Member of the said University or suspected of being such; and in case the said Company, or their Officers or Servants, or any of them, shall not permit such free Access to the said Depots or Stations as aforesaid, or shall not furnish such Information as herein-before mentioned, the said Officer or Servant of the said Company shall for each Default forfeit and pay a sum not exceeding Five Pounds.

CCCV. And be it enacted, That if the said Vice Chancellor or Proctors or Pro-proctors for the Time being of the said University, or Heads of Colleges and Halls, or the Marshal of the said University, or other Person or Persons deputed as aforesaid, shall at any Time or Times previous to the starting of any Train of Carriages upon the said Railway, notify to the proper Officer, Book-keeper, or Servant of the said Company that any Person or Persons about to travel in or upon the said Railway is a Member of the University not having taken the Degree of Master of Arts or Bachelor in Civil Law, and shall identify such Member to such proper Officer, Book-keeper, or Servant of the Company, at the Time of giving such Notice, and require such Officer, Book-keeper, or Servant to decline to take such Member of the University as a Passenger upon the said Railway, the proper Officer, Book-keeper, or Servant of the said Company shall immediately thereupon, and for the Space of Twenty-four Hours after such Notice, Identification, and Requirement, refuse to convey such Member of the said University in or upon the said Railway, and which he is hereby authorized to do, notwithstanding such Member may have paid his Fare; and in case any such Member of the said University shall be knowingly and wilfully allowed to be conveyed thereon after such Notice, within the Time aforesaid, the said Company shall for each Passenger so conveyed forfeit and pay a Sum not exceeding Five Pounds: Provided always, that no Member of the University represented as such to the said Company, or any of their Officers or Servants, by the said Vice Chancellor, Proctors, Pro-proctors, Heads of Colleges and Halls, Marshal, or other Person or Persons deputed as aforesaid, or any of them, who shall be refused to be carried by the said Company, or by any of their Officers or Servants, shall on that account be entitled to claim or recover any Damage or Compensation from the said Company, or such Officers, Book-keepers, or Servants, provided that, in case such Member shall have paid his Fare, the same shall have been tendered or returned to him on Demand.

CCCVI. And be it enacted, That it shall not be lawful for the said Company to take up or set down any Person or Persons being Members of the University, but not having taken the Degree of Master of Arts or Bachelor in Civil Law, on any Part of the said Railway, except at the regularly appointed Stations of the Line; and in case the said Company shall take up or set down any such Person or Persons, except at such regularly appointed Stations of the line, they shall forfeit a

Sum not exceeding Five Pounds for each such Person so taken up or set down.[12]

As railway services increased this degree of control became impossible and, as John Corbin recorded,

the men to whom immorality seems inevitable – and such are to be found in all communities – have recourse to London. But as their expeditions take place in daylight and cold blood, and are, except at great risk, cut short when the last evening train leaves Paddington shortly after dinner, it is not possible to carry them off with that dazzling air of the man of the world that in America lures so many silly freshmen into dissipations for which they have no natural inclination.[13]

Nor was it necessary to travel so far since Mark Tellar was told of a hotel in Reading where

one could without previous notice turn up . . . with a woman, and without luggage; take a private sitting-room and a double bedroom nominally for the night; pay in advance; and, so as to be back in college by midnight, leave by the last train to Oxford.[14]

Such misbehaviour was perhaps uncommon and the proctors' attention was more likely to be focused on drunken, high-spirited undergraduates. G.B. Grundy recalled one such incident:

Two B.N.C. men had been gated for a month in the summer term for coursing at Iffley. To celebrate the end of this period of confinement they invited about twenty men to dinner in their rooms over Loder's Club, opposite University College. I did not like such entertainments, and made an excuse for keeping away. But on the night I was coming back from Magdalen up the High Street just when the whole lot of diners issued into the street. Hilarious they certainly were; but

not intoxicated. One man, an Irishman whom we called Mickey, was however in that state which police call 'having taken liquor,' and was dazed in mind and unsteady on his legs. I got hold of his arm to take him to college, steering him with some difficulty. When we were opposite St. Mary's the cry of 'The proggins (proctor) is coming' was raised, and I saw him with the bulldogs about thirty yards in front of us. I tried to get Mickey to the other side of the street. He flatly refused to come, and mentioned in a loud voice that he did not care a ——— for all the ——— proggins in the kingdom. I crossed to the other side of the street, having no desire to be caught in such compromising company. I waited there and watched to see what happened to Mickey. What did happen horrified me. When the proctor got close to him Mickey thought I had come back, threw his arms round the proctor's neck and kissed him, remarking in a loud tone 'Good old chap, I knew you would not desert me. They told me the ——— proggins was coming.' The bulldogs disentangled the proctor from Mickey's embrace, and led the offender off in custody.[15]

Within the colleges, there was of course much scope for wild behaviour. Here, James Pycroft describes 'the rowing or uproarious set, who behaved like big schoolboys':

These were the men who made night hideous with drunken and noisy wine parties – men who knocked in late and bribed the Porter not to put down their names. Among these the most conspicuous were Charlie Lane and Tom Briggs. . . . Charlie was a clever fellow, but all brain and excitement, and Tom was a man of peculiar capacity. In the winners of the Derby or St. Leger his memory was remarkable; but as to the dates of kings and queens he was nowhere. Indeed, it was said that he thought the battle of Blenheim was fought in Woodstock Park! Charlie might have done anything in point of talent, but his mind was like a sharp weapon loose in the handle, he was too restless and excitable to fix his attention to

'*A College Wine*' *in progress at the turn of the century. With the drink flowing freely, it was not unusual for such parties to end in riotous confusion and a sobering interview with the head of the college.*

any subject for many minutes together. Charlie was one of the many lunatics at large – men who only do not count as mad because they are not mischievous, but men whose brains are subject to a periodical effervescence, and who at times are no more answerable for their words than a barrel-organ is for the tunes it shall play.[16]

Some of this effervescence was evident in 1863 when the colleges were hit by a craze for tilting with chairs:

This tilting mania was, in my opinion, the swiftest and most absorbing mental epidemic that has ever overrun a city. Men really seemed to think and talk of nothing but their tourna-ments, and every object was referred to one single standard. We all know how a sporting man (not a sportsman) looks upon every event as a vehicle for betting, how a naval man measures everything by nautical rule, and how a mathemati-cian wants to turn every idea into a proposition. Thus did the unfortunates who were bitten by this tarantula learn to look upon chairs and sofas merely according to their capabilities in a tilting match; any smooth and hard patch of road was imme-diately pounced upon as *such* a sweet spot for a tournament, and the merits and demerits of mutual acquaintance were all weighed in the same balance.

One man would ask another, 'What do you think of Smith, of Ch. Ch.?' to whom he had just been introduced, and would probably get for answer, 'Oh! he's not much good; Jones on my staircase would knock him over like ninepins.' Or perhaps the opinion might be more favourable – 'Smith of Ch. Ch.? First-rate! Saw him cut over half-a-dozen of our men without giving them a chance.' Or perhaps the opinion might run thus:– 'What do I think of Smith? Why, I think he has the best chair in the 'Varsity'.[17]

Sporting achievements often inspired over-enthusiastic celebrations and, in February 1883, Lewis Farnell witnessed the scene in

Brasenose College quad after the Torpid crew had gone Head of the River:

In the flickering light of the bonfires thoughtfully arranged by the edge of the grass could be seen the figures of some two hun-dred young men bounding and leaping high round the images and passing from lurid light into deep shadow alternately; and the leaping was accompanied by terrifying yells and the most fantastic music ever devised by savages standing on the verge of culture; for every one of the participants had equipped himself with his flat-bottomed bath – part of an undergraduate's outfit before college bathrooms were built: this he held in his left hand and his sitting-room poker in his right, and by banging it on the centre of his bath he produced sounds which, multiplied by two hundred others chiming in, might well surpass the same number of bull-roarers in volume and terror. When the tone of the bath was injured by the poker going through the bottom as frequently happened, the dancer threw it away and was immediately sup-plied with a new one by one of the scouts who stood around in an admiring group away from the inner circle.[18]

The aftermath of a college Rag was described by Henry Kingsley in his Oxford novel RAVENSHOE:

It was nine o'clock on the 6th of November. The sun was shining aslant into two pretty little Gothic windows in the inner or library quadrangle of St. Paul's College, and illumi-nating the features of a young man who was standing in the middle of the room scratching his head. . . . He stood in his shirt and trousers only, in the midst of a scene of desolation so awful, that I who have had to describe some of the most terri-ble scenes and circumstances conceivable, pause before attempting to give any idea of it in black and white. Every moveable article in the room – furniture, crockery, fender, fire-irons – lay in one vast heap of broken confusion in the corner of the room. Not a pane of glass remained in the win-dows; the bedroom-door was broken down; and the door which opened into the corridor was minus the two upper panels.

The Dean sarcastically congratulated Charles Ravenshoe that 'Your career at the University has been brilliant; but your orbit being highly elliptical, it is to be feared that you will remain but a short time above the horizon'. He was subsequently rusticated for a year.[19] After a real-life incident in 1894, fifteen members of the Bullingdon Club were sent down for allegedly breaking no fewer than 460 windows in Peckwater Quad, Christ Church. There was some criticism of the light sentence and An Oxonian of The Old Days objected that:

their departure is the occasion for a splendid ovation of rowdy University enthusiasm. A mob of townsmen and gownsmen accompany them to the station, their cabs being 'drawn by men in cap and gown with the Bullingdon favours', the whole station is in an uproar, the train delayed a quarter of an hour till the scene is ended, and the 'sent down' depart amid the cheers of hundreds.

Is not this rather a curious scene, Sir, for a college or a University which used to pride itself on its gentlemanly character?. . . If such is to be the behaviour and discipline of a large number of young men, many or most of them of the richer or higher ranks of life, how can we reproach the lower classes for their strikes, their violence, or their indifference to authority?[20]

After an earlier outrage at Christ Church in 1870 when undergraduates removed statues from the college library and made a bonfire around them, the Dean, Henry Liddell, expressed the difficulties which the authorities faced in dealing with wealthy vandals:

Young men of large fortune have little to fear from such penalties as we can impose. . . . The late Lord Lyttelton, who turned out a very steady, useful man, was the first who painted the Dean's Door. The late Lord Derby is believed to have been the ringleader of a party who pulled down the figure which still gives name to the fountain in the Great

Verdant Green attends college chapel, his presence being noted by two men who 'quickly pricked a mark against his name on the chapel lists'. Chapel attendance was compulsory and, for many undergraduates, it was a disciplinary rather than a spiritual experience.

Quadrangle. The attack in my garden last summer . . . was led by two noble Lords, one of whom had never been a member of any University, the other did not belong to us but had graduated with honour from a College of high repute in the University and actually held, as he still holds, the position of a Lord of Her Majesty's Treasury.

Can it be a matter of surprise that, when such things receive such countenance, there should be individuals in each successive generation of wealthy undergraduates who think it a noble pastime to imitate and improve upon the freaks of their predecessors?[21]

A wintry view of No. 17 St Margaret's Road, a rather plain semi-detached house built in 1875. When this photograph was taken in the 1890s, it was the home of Robert Barrett, a man of independent means, who lived there with his wife, his sister-in-law and one servant.

CHAPTER SIX

North Oxford

S T JUDE'S COLLEGE had been devastated, more than almost any other, by the scourge of matrimony. Fellow after Fellow had been swept away into the 'Parks system' by this deadly scourge, and lived their blameless lives in little red houses with a cat-walk behind, and a perambulator and a bicycle on either side of the front door.[1]

North Oxford tends to be seen as a one-class suburb built after 1877 for the new generation of married fellows.

In fact development of the area began in the 1820s and was far from homogeneous. Substantial homes were built for the Oxford iron-monger, J.S. Browning, the town clerk, G.P. Hester and Thomas Mallam, an auctioneer who had formerly been a tobacconist. Their estates were called respectively Northgate House, The Mount and The Shrubbery, but local wags nicknamed them Tinville, Quillville and Quidville. Away to the west, however, an iron foundry, a boat build-ing dock and other canal-side industries introduced a small labouring population. To the north, Summertown provided sites for countrified estates, small villas and labourers' cottages, creating pockets of poverty within yards of the gates of the wealthy.

Two major developments in the mid-nineteenth century threatened to destroy the suburb's social status before it was truly established. In 1850, the Oxford Board of Guardians bought a site off Banbury Road for a new workhouse and, in 1851, the Oxford, Worcester and Wolverhampton Railway was planning a railway line across North Oxford.[2] Neither scheme came to fruition and the Guardians' site was sold off to become Park Town, a 'new and salubrious suburb' designed by the local architect Samuel Lipscomb Seckham. The OXFORD UNIVERSITY & CITY GUIDE remarked:

Nothing can more clearly show the worth of such an addition to Oxford, than the speed with which each house has met with occupants, it being within a few minutes walk from the centre of Oxford, the Parks, and the University Museum.[3]

The building of Park Town prompted St John's College to obtain an Act of Parliament in 1855 enabling it to grant ninety-nine-year building leases over its extensive North Oxford estate. The develop-ment of Norham Manor from 1860 proved attractive to professors and heads of houses who were already allowed to marry; the first two houses were occupied by Professors of History, Goldwin Smith and Montagu Burrows.

Many of the villas in this new suburb were, however, occupied by professional people, successful businessmen and men and women of independent means. Married tutors provided a further impetus to development from the later 1870s, but towards the Oxford Canal North Oxford remained more Town than Gown. In 1890, the com-mittee asking for a grant towards the building of St Margaret's church expressed the fear that

their application may seem to some almost indecent as coming from a parish which contains so many new roads of villas. But they would venture to submit that very many inhabitants are birds of passage and few are wealthy.[4]

The proposed Oxford, Worcester and Wolverhampton Railway station in North Oxford in 1851. This bird's eye view clearly shows the Woodstock and Banbury Roads and a cluster of houses in North Parade, a small freehold estate developed in the 1830s.

The domestic Gothic houses of North Oxford were in the forefront of architectural fashion and developers tried to give each one a bespoke character, varying the accommodation and design 'to meet as far as possible the requirements of different householders'.[5] The richest elements of the middle class were not easily satisfied and, in 1884, Professor E.B. Poulton wrote to St John's about extending the six-bedroomed Wykeham House in Banbury Road:

The college perhaps thinks that the house is large. They do not consider how long it has been vacant at various times – simply on account of its insufficient accommodation. I constantly meet people who tell me that they have thought of it but did not take it on this account. . . . It is therefore obvious that the house is inadequate for even a small family. . . .[6]

Naomi Mitchison has described the accommodation at No. 4 St Margaret's Road, a big detached house built in 1884:

There was a great big brass knob on the front door, a circular space in front which we called a drive, and a wide wooden gate on which I was not supposed to swing, with almond trees at both sides. There was also a basement with kitchen, scullery, a servants' WC. . . . The whole basement was dark, lit from a front area which enclosed the windows almost totally and a back area with a slope of rubble or stone on the garden side. . . . On the ground floor you went through to the garden; the stairs went straight up and down. There was a largish drawing-room, a study, a dining-room, perhaps a pantry at the head of the back stairs down to the basement, and certainly a gentleman's lavatory. All this was standard in a detached house of the period. There were, rather surprisingly, two bathrooms, one of them rather scruffy, and there was also a water closet with a bottom pan opening down into darkness and smell. This probably induced constipation in everybody.[7]

John and Louisa Haldane, moving into No. 11 Crick Road, also suspected the sanitary arrangements, but

There were two Burne-Jones lights in the drawing-room bay window, and the dining-room opened into a perfectly charming little garden, which must have been carved out of an old orchard. It was half-filled with the best bearing apple trees I have ever had to deal with.[8]

In general, most North Oxford residents would probably have agreed with Myfanwy Rhys who, in 1884, found her new home, No. 43 Banbury Road, 'very convenient and pretty'.[9] Mrs Humphry Ward recalled the lifestyle of the new suburbanites:

We had many friends, all pursuing the same kind of life as ourselves and interested in the same kind of things. Nobody under the rank of a head of a college, except a very few privileged professors, possessed as much as a thousand a year. The average income of the new race of married tutor was not much more than half that sum. Yet we all gave dinner-parties and furnished our houses with Morris papers, old chests and cabinets, and blue pots. The dinner parties were simple and short. At our own early efforts of the kind there certainly was not enough to eat. But we all improved with time; and on the whole I think we were very fair housekeepers and competent mothers. Most of us were very anxious to be up-to-date and in the fashion, whether in aesthetics, in housekeeping or education. But our fashion was not that of Belgravia or Mayfair, which indeed we scorned! It was the fashion of the movement which sprang from Morris and Burne-Jones. Liberty stuffs, very plain in line, but elaborately 'smocked' were greatly in

vogue, and evening dresses 'cut square', or with 'Watteau pleats' were generally worn, and often in conscious protest against the London 'low dress' which Oxford – young married Oxford – thought both 'ugly' and 'fast'. And when we had donned our Liberty gowns we went out to dinner, the husband walking, the wife in a bath chair, drawn by an ancient member of an ancient and close fraternity – the 'chairmen' of old Oxford.[10]

Elizabeth Wordsworth wrote to her sister-in-law, Esther, imagining the hectic preparations for a North Oxford dinner party:

As I write John is (let us hope) going down to the cellar after his best claret, and you are putting ivy-leaves from Wytham into the dessert dates and crystallised fruit, and Ada Burson is doing up for herself some little bit of finery in which blue ribbon is the chief ingredient, and the great guns who shall be nameless are saying what a bore it is to have to dine with college tutors and their wives.[11]

Louisa Haldane found the dinner parties given by the Burdon-Sandersons

The least sociable that it has ever been my lot to attend. The dinners were long and solid, the room got fearfully hot and stuffy, and their dogs were often not in the best of health. I usually had 'Uncle John' on one side of me and on the other some elderly scientist who tried to produce light conversation. If either of them said anything which made me laugh, everybody looked up and someone said hopefully, 'Oh, do tell us what that was', and the poor joke fell dead. After dinner we women were arranged carefully in pairs round the drawing-room. You never got the chance of picking your partner, and if by good luck you started a conversation with your neighbour, it was sure to be interrupted – not by the men! (they sat on endlessly and John used to come in yawning and looking a picture of misery) – but Aunt Ghetal conscientiously broke up the couples she had arranged so that one had sometimes started

Woodstock Road, looking north from the Horse and Jockey pub in about 1870. On the right, overgrown hedges from pre-existing fields contrast with the recently completed Gothic buildings of the Holy Trinity Convent. Further north, St Philip and St James' church had been erected between 1862 and 1866.

The Barrett family picnicking by the Cherwell in the 1890s. The upper river was the exclusive preserve of a few North Oxford families with access to boats until 1901 when Thomas Tims began to hire out punts and other boats on the site of the Cherwell Boathouse.

the same subject with six or seven different ladies by the end of the evening.[12]

In 1893, Myfanwy Rhys and her sister Olwen were no more impressed by lunch at the Wallaces:

Another person there whom we gradually perceived to be connected with Lynham's school, I took rather an objection to her. Olwen thought that she was schoolmissy to the last extreme and tried to pat everyone on the head. Luncheon was good, conversation the reverse. Mr Wallace's speech was limited to one or two observations such as that he had lost all appetite for breakfast and so forth. Mrs Wallace kept dribbling on, for Miss Bagnell's (I think this was her name) benefit Isa said nothing, O said nothing, I said nothing. . . .[13]

Calling on friends became something of a ritual for many North Oxford ladies, and Louisa Haldane was furious when her parlour-maid hid many visiting cards because she thought 'I had far more visitors than was good for me'.[14] In 1898, Myfanwy Rhys recorded a particularly unsuccessful afternoon's visiting:

Went out calling with Mamma. Called on Popes, Traceys, Haldanes, Charles, Sweets, Pagets, Sandays, Drivers, Clauds, Pelhams, Wards, all out, and Cheynes in, Mrs Cheyne seems pleasant though cut and dried. Dorothy has been house-keeping lately, looks very pleasant.[15]

Ethel Hatch's mother, like many hostesses, held a weekly 'At Home' when visitors called for tea; occasionally, she staged afternoon receptions when musical friends entertained the company with songs and violin or piano solos after tea or coffee in the dining room.[16] Music-making was very popular and, in June 1891 for instance, a Mr Dixon came for coffee at the Lucys,

brought his flute and played and sang to us; in October, Catherine's younger sister Edith, played the newly delivered

piano after dinner and a visitor in November played the mandolin.[17]

In summer, the North Oxford garden provided a secluded adjunct to the house, a place for parties, games and quiet recreation. In her novel BELINDA, Rhoda Broughton has the girls

Beginning the day with a preliminary saunter round the narrow bounds of the little garden, and the newly-mown tennis-ground. They are very small bounds, but within them is room for undried dew; for a blackbird with a voice a hundred times bigger than its body; for a guelder rose, a fine broom-bush, and a short-lived lilac.[18]

Though comparatively small, such gardens provided the privacy beloved of middle-class Victorians and they helped to create the illusion of a country estate; indeed, William Wilkinson, architect to the St John's College estate from 1860, illustrated four North Oxford houses in his book ENGLISH COUNTRY HOUSES, first published in 1870. The spring-time display of flowering trees and shrubs had become worthy of comment by the 1880s and, in 1897, proud owners — through their gardeners — vied with each other in providing colourful front gardens:

A stroll along the Banbury or Woodstock Roads at the present time would reveal a large number of very choice groups of border tulips, narcise, & c. (the hyacinths being past their best); but at Cross Ways Mr M. Wootten has a bed of fifteen hundred tulips, which are a centre of attraction to passers-by. Five varieties only are employed, arranged in double curving lines (one hundred and fifty in each row), the *tout ensemble* forming a colour picture worthy the pencil of an artist, and Mr J. Clarke, the gardener, may be fairly congratulated on his success in blending the varieties. In the course of a week there will be a fine collection of florists' tulips, and soon the tulip beds will be filled with zonal geraniums and tuberous begonias, Mr Wootten possessing, perhaps, the largest collection of the last named in the district.[19]

Croquet in the garden of No. 13 Norham Gardens, illustrated in William Wilkinson's book English Country Houses *in 1875. Built in 1868–70, the house was on the show front of the Norham Manor estate with extensive views over the newly-formed University Parks.*

The North Oxford lifestyle was underpinned by a veritable army of domestic servants. As Naomi Mitchison recalled:

Oxford servants were much discussed in drawing-rooms. If one didn't have some kind of local source, like farmers' daughters, whom one might know something about, then there was nothing for it but a registry office. Then there was the business of written references and reading between the lines. What had been left out? Ladies were often asked for references for someone who had been with them years before, if, say, the most recent employer had died.[20]

In 1908, Mrs Burton of Luton provided this reference for Carmen Welch who was seeking a position with Mrs Collier of 224 Woodstock Road in Oxford:

I found her to be honest, clean, willing and quite trustworthy.

I cannot say if she would wake with an alarum clock as we always called her at six. . . .

You will find her quite capable of taking charge of plain cooking etc. when necessary, although she is not so fond of cooking as of general housework and care of children. . . .

I always allowed her one evening out each week and once on Sunday.

She is fairly strong and healthy so far as I know, but it would not be advisable to work her too hard.[21]

In 1894, Myfanwy Rhys' mother was 'terribly worried about the new housemaid who is a moke and will have to move on. I could not get her to take much interest in anything'. Four years later, the family faced a brief crisis:

Sunday. The servants struck – the housemaid would not be debarred from the rites of public worship. The peevish parlour-maid said she was not going to stay in, nor was Sandford. The other two had gone out in due course so there it was. While we were in chapel Mother had to go and bring coal up from the cellar. Father and the R(andells) dined in hall. Supper. O and I put our feet down and would *not* allow Mother to clear the table.[22]

Under the headline 'Silver Spoons in the Dust Cart' the OXFORD TIMES *in January 1889 reported:*

The carelessness which characterises the domestic servant is shown by one of a series of incidents which has just occurred in North Oxford. A Local Board dustman, named Kitchen, was removing house refuse in that district on Monday last, and in emptying his cart discovered two silver table-spoons among the house refuse . . . Kitchen at once took his 'find' to the Police-station, where the spoons await identification by the owner, who, no doubt, will reward the honest fellow, and soundly rate the domestic.[23]

Surrounded by luxury and on very low wages, domestic servants were beset by temptations and it is not surprising that a few succumbed. Thus, in May 1882, two of Professor Pritchard's servants at No. 8 Keble Terrace were accused of stealing a watch and trinkets and one was found guilty.[24]

The North Oxford house set in its leafy garden would seem to have been a perfect example of the Englishman's castle, but the reality did not always conform to this image. In the first place, neighbours were kept at a distance, but they still managed to intrude. At Poynings House in Woodstock Road, for instance, Professor Holland was upset in 1882 by 'a substantial fowl-house' that was being built next door by the editor of the OXFORD TIMES, George Rippon;[25] in 1892, Walter Gray was told by St John's College to remove a school at No. 34 St Margaret's Road because it was termed 'a serious nuisance'.[26] Dr James Murray, the editor of the OXFORD ENGLISH DICTIONARY, made a very discreet complaint to the City in September 1898:

I am very unwilling to lodge a complaint against a neighbour; and yet I feel obliged to call your attention to the serious annoyance caused by the burning of damp weeds and green garden rubbish on the grounds of 'the Mount' opposite to my house. . . . Often a dense blue-white smoke comes percolating through the trees and over the fence, the whole day over, as has been the case today, filling the atmosphere round my house, and entering the house through open windows, doors and ventilators, to the great offence of the nose and eyes. Today it has penetrated into my Scriptorium through the door and ventilating windows, and made my work highly unpleasant. . . . I would be glad if this Authority would ask (or order) Mr Hartley or his gardener to desist from the practice, as having been the subject of complaint by surrounding residents, without expressly naming *me*, if this can be done, and merely as a matter of public order and police.[27]

At No. 4 St Margaret's Road, Naomi Mitchison was not allowed to climb into the next door garden because the neighbours were

Liberals,[28] but these political differences were perhaps eclipsed by the so-called 'cat-astrophy' case of June 1899 in Oxford County Court. Here, Victor Veley of 20 Bradmore Road tried — unsuccessfully — to obtain damages from Mrs Toynbee of No. 10 Norham Gardens because of injuries suffered by his Royal Siamese cat:

Victor Herbert Veley, MA, FRS, then gave evidence. It appeared that he lived at 20 Bradmore Road. Plaintiff was in his garden on May 22, about 3.45 pm, when defendant's cat came over the wall from defendant's garden and flew at his animal. Plaintiff attempted to drive the animal away, and eventually the intruder went back witness's cat following.

His Honour: Do I understand that they had one round in your garden and they then went and had round number two in defendant's garden? (Laughter)
Plaintiff: Yes. . .
In answer to cross-examination by Mr Mallam, witness said he did not see the fight continued on the greenhouse in defendant's garden, and he did not know whether any of these cuts were caused by glass.
Mr Mallam: They have had these little busts before?
Yes. (Laughter)
It is not usual for Tom-cats to fight?
His Honour: Yes. (Laughter).[29]

Crime, or the fear of it, provided a second and more serious threat to the enjoyment of a peaceful suburban life. G..P Hester, living at The Mount on Banbury Road, thought it necessary to carry a gun on his way home at night [30] while Gordon Dayman, another solicitor living further north at Cherwell Croft, arranged a police escort through the trees north of Park Town.[31] On winter evenings in 1872 North Oxford was said to be 'infested with beggars, who if not relieved became very insolent';[32] in 1893, Myfanwy Rhys visited another house and found everyone 'in a state. They had had a scare with a tramp, who had not taken anything however.'[33] A serious outbreak of vandalism in North Oxford gardens in 1880 led to determined police action:

The bosky surroundings of The Firs, No. 31 Banbury Road, which was designed by William Wilkinson, the architect to the St John's College estate, and built in 1866. The college insisted on low garden walls and railings on its estate, but judicious planting soon ensured a high degree of privacy.

It appears that in consequence of the damage, constables in plain clothes were placed on duty in different parts of the north of Oxford. After PC Fundell had been secreted in Mr Cousin's garden about an hour, he saw Clarke enter and pull up a shrub, and he then seized him. Savage, who was near him, ran away.

The two lads, caught, perhaps appropriately, in the garden of 'Shrublands', Banbury Road, were sent to prison for a month.[34]

Burglars were a more intractable problem in the suburb not only because 'the large residences . . . afford ample scope for their nefarious designs' but also because many properties were unoccupied during the Long Vacation. Thus, in September 1861, a Park Town house was broken into in broad daylight while the household was at the seaside and, in 1897, the Revd L.J.M. Bebb, Fellow of Brasenose, even went to the trouble of leaving a notice on the front door of No. 96 Banbury Road informing the world that he was on holiday in Bournemouth.[35] At times, the threat of burglaries created almost a siege mentality as Olwen Rhys recorded in September 1897:

I expect we shall very soon be going to bed – I already hear a locking-up voyage going around the house – Mrs Morfill has alarmed us by burglary tales – Mr Bebb's house, Mr Seary's in the Crescent and others have been robbed while shut up.[36]

The difficulties faced by North Oxford residents were but a minor blemish in a privileged lifestyle which less well-placed Oxonians could scarcely help envying. Henry Taunt, the Oxford photographer living in unfashionable Cowley Road, summed up these feelings in the poem OXFORD, FROM THE ORDNANCE SURVEY:

> The Map of Oxford forms an Ass,
>   Much burdened with a heavy load,
> And thus with all the rates to pass,
>   The rider has a sharpen'd goad;
> For this much smaller uppish class,
>   North Oxford, rides the Oxford Ass.[37]

CHAPTER SEVEN

Employment

In the sad and sodden street,
    To and fro
Flit the fever-stricken feet
    Of the freshers as they meet,
Come and go,
    Ever buying, buying, buying,
When the shopmen stand supplying,
    Vying, vying
    All they know,
While the Autumn lies a-dying
    Sad and low.[1]

Many Oxford tradesmen relied heavily on University custom and were genuinely delighted by the arrival of each year's batch of freshmen. The fictional Verdant Green followed a typical route around the city's shops and livery stables, taking in the papier mâché souvenirs at Spiers and Son's well-known establishment in High Street. Here, he ordered

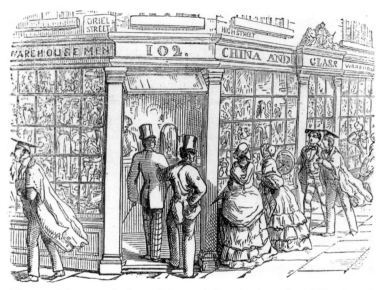

The noted fancy goods shop, Spiers and Son, in the early 1850s. Famed especially for its papier mâché articles and Oxford souvenirs, this shop flourished on the corner of High Street and Oriel Street from 1835 to 1889.

a fire-screen to be prepared with the family-arms, as a present for his father; a ditto, with the view of his college, for his mother; a writing-case, with the High Street view, for his aunt; a netting-box, card-case, and a model of the Martyrs' Memorial, for his three sisters; and having thus bountifully remembered his family circle; he treated himself with a modest paper-knife, and was treated in return by Mr Spiers with a perfect bijou of art, in the shape of 'a memorial for visitors to

Oxford', in which the chief glories of that city were set forth in gold and colours, in the most attractive form, and which our hero immediately posted off to the Manor Green.[2]

The credit system was almost universal in the Oxford shops and James Pycroft's spendthrift undergraduate, Belton, was rapidly accumulating a mountain of debt:

Cooks working in New College kitchen in June 1901. College service was a major employer in Oxford, but many men were left idle during the University vacations.

On wet and dreary days, when there was nothing doing, Belton would wrap his gown about his shoulders, and lounge about the town, amusing himself with those most expensive of all sights, which are to be seen for nothing in shop windows. One while he would walk into the saddler's and ask about the next Meet, and, though he never intended it, leave a girth, curb chain, or currycomb memorandum, by which he would be able to know exactly the day on which he made the inquiry. He would then turn into the jeweller's to have his ring cleaned, or watch regulated, – to the picture dealer's to see the last HB, or some new drawing of the winner of St Leger or a steeple chase. So, also, ice, cherry brandy, or oyster patties at the confectioner's; a new pair of gloves or fancy handkerchief at the hatter's; a walking stick, or some of the thousand and one tempting articles at the shop of the perfumer who monopolises the corner – would all be something to do.[3]

The scale of these debts could be astonishing and in 1848, one undergraduate, Edward Jennings, owed sixty-eight Oxford tradesmen a total of £1063 2s. 2d after three years of 'reckless extravagance'.[4] Oxford tradesmen were sometimes blamed for operating on credit, but it was clearly impossible for any one individual to draw back from a system which stimulated demand in every branch of trade. They were also accused of over-charging but, as Stedman remarked,

Many men think nothing of keeping a tradesman waiting for years for his money. Tradesmen cannot live on hope and promises, and they are forced to make the possessor of ready cash pay for the delinquencies of the Skimpoles of the University.[5]

Colleges were major employers in Oxford and, in 1901, 609 men were described as being engaged in college or club service.[6] Most college servants were not well paid and they relied to some extent upon gratuities from undergraduates. John Corbin discovered that

All broken bread, meat and wine are his perquisites, and tradition allows him to 'bag' a fair amount of tea, coffee, and sugar.

Out of all this he makes a sumptuous living. I knew only one exception, and that was when four out of six men on a certain scout's staircase happened to be vegetarians, and five teetotallers. The poor fellow was in extremities for meat and in desperation for drink.[7]

Edward Thomas's scout was luckier or perhaps more skilled in his choice of staircase:

He awakens you every morning by playing with your bath, and is a perpetually recurring background to the sweet disquiet of your last half-hour in bed. In serving you, he serves himself; and late in the day he is to be seen with a wallet on his back, bent under such 'learning's crumbs' as half-empty winebottles and jars of Cooper's marmalade. In these matters he has a neat running hand, without flourishes. No man has the air of being so much as he the right hand of fate. When he drinks your wine and disappoints a joyous company, when he assumes your best cigars, and leaves only those which were provided for the freshman of taste – so inevitable are his ways that you can only hope sarcastically that he liked the fare. He appears to have a noble scorn of cash, when he asks for it; and you are bound to imitate. All the wisdom of the wise is cheap compared with his manner of beginning a speech with, 'If you please, sir, it is usual for freshmen to, . . .' while he is dusting your photographs. He is blessed with an incapacity to blush.[8]

The University Press in Walton Street was an important centre of labour with 278 employees in 1883.[9] In 1865, the press was forced to defend itself against charges that it exploited the 120 boys who worked there. They began work at the age of twelve and were said to have ample opportunities for recreation and continuing education:

The hours of work are from 6 am to half-past 8 am from 9 am to 1 pm, and from 2 pm to 6 pm, in all 10 hours and a half. Saturday is a half holiday, on which day the boys work only until 1 pm, making the total working hours of the week 59, from which about 8 hours should be deducted for the half hours' play in the back yard, which every boy gets daily while his machine is being made ready, and for other reasons, making the average of the day's work through the week under 9 hours and a half.[10]

In the 1870s, School Board byelaws made it impossible to employ children of school age and, in 1876, Pickard Hall announced that the Press 'had been obliged to employ young women in the warehouse.'[11]

Varsity custom helped to support many specialized crafts and on 17 January, 1885, for example, C.F. Cholmondeley, an undergraduate at New College, 'Went up Cowley Road and got a bat from Pether'; in June, he was off to Medley to order a boat from Beesley's for the family pond at Adlestrop.[12] Graduates might continue to patronize such firms in later life and, in April 1855, the OXFORD CHRONICLE announced:

CRICKET IN THE CRIMEA – Mr W. Bacon of Oxford has just sent to the Crimea, six cricket bats, eight balls and two sets of wickets, to the order of Captain Dewar, who is with the army in the Crimea. This shows that the national character of the Englishman for his amusements will become manifest under any circumstance.[13]

Oxford Men also helped to broadcast the reputation of Frank Cooper's Oxford Marmalade which was first made on a domestic scale in 1874 but required factory production by 1903.[14]

Taking in lodgers provided a welcome supplementary income and there were 579 licensed University lodging-houses in Oxford by 1899.[15] During term-time, the University offered an almost unlimited range of casual jobs, whether as charwomen, hairdressers, errand boys, grounds boys or newspaper sellers; even vagrants were drawn to Oxford at the beginning of each term by the prospect of rich pickings from undergraduates.[16]

The University was only up for twenty-four weeks of the year and Oxford had few other major employers. In 1851, Samuel Sidney rejoiced that 'Oxford is so decorously clean, so spotlessly free from the

The Varsity Bat, a prominent advertisement for H.R. Pether's products, outside his Cowley Road cricket bat factory in about 1900. Piles of roughly hewn bats bear witness to the anticipated level of demand from Oxford undergraduates.

Floods on the line in November 1875; Great Western Railway employees struggle to restore train services north of Red Bridge on the Abingdon Road.

smoke of engines and the roar of machinery'.[17] Hall's and Morrell's breweries were said to employ about 150 men in 1876[18] and Oxford's largest building firm, Kingerlee's, had a workforce of between 200 and 300 in the later 1880s.[19] The railway companies employed 451 men by 1901[20] and might have taken on many more if the Great Western Railway Company's proposal to establish a large carriage factory in the city in 1865 had come to fruition. Welcomed by the city and a few University figures, the scheme was, however, generally opposed within the University and the factory was eventually located in Swindon. Professor Goldwin Smith was a leading opponent and drew this angry response from ' A Citizen' in June 1865:

Some of our University authorities manifest great alarm at smoky chimneys and working men being brought within half a mile of this city. 'Smoke' and 'working men' (according to to-day's *Times*) are two horrors, not to come near 'colleges and students'. Well, really Professor G. Smith and the *Times* must be already beclouded if they think that the citizens of Oxford and the public cannot see through the hollowness of their arguments and set them down as all smoke.

I, for one, desire to interpret for them. Instead of smoke, read independence, and instead of working men, read freemen, and then you have the key to unlock opposition raised against the Great Western Railway Company's factory. . . .

Then there is another important movement in the item. Look at 5000 ready money customers all the year round! Our Oxford tradesmen would feel more independent; for, after all, Oxford tradesmen groan under long credit, abuse, and often loss, and would prefer ready money, small profits, and quick returns. . . .

What if the atmosphere of Oxford were a little darkened by a few chimneys, when the wind blew from NW, if the social, commercial, and perhaps the moral atmosphere were cleared by the new element. Surely it would be more healthful, and, if certain morbid minds dread the former more than rejoicing in the latter, all right minded men hail with welcome the 5000 mechanics, chimneys and all.[21]

In the absence of large-scale industrialization, Victorian Oxford enjoyed a permanent demand for goods and services from neighbouring towns and villages and, increasingly, from its own burgeoning suburbs. Carriers' carts and market vans brought goods and people into the city every week and innumerable individuals made regular visits, bringing a few livestock, provisions or hand-made goods to sell and returning with purchases of food, clothing or necessary items. The growing railway network confirmed the city's position at the centre of its region and also made Oxford more accessible for settlement by retired people and the moderately prosperous. The potential of this city and county trade was illustrated by the meteoric career of G.R. Cooper who came to Oxford in about 1866, set up an ironmongery business in St Ebbe's and was able to retire to a large house in Boar's Hill, having laid the foundations of one of Oxford's department stores.[22] A correspondent for the DRAPERS' TRADE JOURNAL visited Oxford in 1873 and found the streets

fairly bristling with vehicles, commodities, round plump red faces, antiquated garments, heavy boots and ugly bonnets, while the quiet still air resounded with all kinds of gossip.

Almost directly after I had cleared the station, I came upon an old friend, in Mr Bell, but the only thing I shall say of him is that he is a philanthropist, who is making every effort to provide tasty bonnets at low prices for the plebeians of Oxon, in place of the ugly old straws, and still uglier old print sun-bonnets . . . which is the general order of an old countrywoman when she requires a replacement of the one that has, mayhap, served her for the past two years. I am sure that, if they pass Mr Bell's, a radical change will soon be effected. In Castle-street, Mr Johnson is selling off previous to retirement. . . . For the window I cannot, of course, say much – a mixture of whitening, umbrellas, posters, and various other goods, is not generally considered to be a mark of window-dressing talent, although it is like a loadstone to a needle with the bargain-hunting old tabs that form a moderate proportion of country women. . . .

Showroom Staff Xmas 1908

The showroom staff of F. Cape & Co., at Christmas in 1908. Shopwork provided respectable employment for women and girls and larger stores like Capes, the drapers, offered living accommodation for their employees.

I continued to Magdalen street where Elliston's, as they are called 'for short', or, to give them their full title, Elliston, Cavell, and Son, are undoubtedly the premiers of the trade at Oxford, and are blessed with an extensive connection amongst county families. A very pretty lobby has of late been erected as an entrance to the costume and millinery show rooms, and the effect of the whole, with its pretty decorations, is good in the extreme.[23]

Elliston's and other fashionable shops benefited hugely from the spending power of North Oxford ladies. Myfanwy Rhys recorded this shopping expedition with Miss Lorenz in her diary for 1898:

I toddled forth with her and a regular *Bataille des Dames* was enacted on the Drapery stage. With difficulty did we escape from Elliston without our having committed ourselves to the purchase of a jacket priced £7.7 with no end of sable etc. Badcock was more phlegmatic and there was a drop to £1.5. This did not do and she decided to have a costume and buy a mantle of fur. We finally paid a visit to Frank East. Here we took advantage of the temporary distraction of the staff to try on all the available jackets. When we had decided to our satisfaction that they were all made in Germany and would not do, we were set upon by the shop walker who tried to force a coat and skirt on us.[24]

These shops became substantial employers, particularly of women, but 'One who Serves' complained bitterly about living and working conditions in 1899. The shop girl had to work long hours for perhaps 5s. a week

with the mind continually on the strain serving customers . . . a shop girl has always to speak civilly and respectfully, and to maintain an amiable demeanour to a lady who will trouble her to show her all her stock, and then often . . . walk out of the shop without buying a single thing'.

Furthermore, the food and accommodation for assistants who lived on the premises might be appalling with

three or four, more often five and even six . . . stuffed into a bedroom, with no convenience for women as regards having anywhere to put their clothes. One small chest of drawers does duty for all, no places to hang their dresses, etc., and worst of all only one wash stand.[25]

Domestic service and the clothing industry were the other major employers of women and girls in Victorian Oxford. In 1901, 3,920 females were engaged as domestic servants in Oxford[26] and according to a correspondent in 1897, their average working day began at 6 a.m. or 6.30 a.m., continuing until 10, 11 or 12 in the evening:

It is hard work, too, a good deal of upstairs work, with perhaps the luxury of three hours off once in the week, and the same luxury on the glorious Sabbath, for the immense sum of 3s a week.[27]

Women in the clothing industry worked in large factories such as Hyde's in Queen Street and Lucas's in George Street although many more were employed as outworkers in their own homes. One such was Bessie Haycroft in St Thomas's who wrote to Christ Church in January 1898, attempting unsuccessfully to have her rent reduced. She worked for Hyde's, but her wage

does not come on average to more than 12/- a week and often it is very much less than that. Our rent is 4/2 a week, and my father's advancing years, and the work becoming more and more difficult for me we are very anxious for the future. I have to work from early morning till late at night to earn such a living as we have . . .[28]

Oxford was at the heart of a low pay area and for much of the workforce, employment depended not only upon the weather and the time of year but also upon the presence or absence of the University. In 1859, the City and University established a scheme by which some college servants found employment in holiday resorts during the Long Vacation; they were thus saved from 'idleness and thoughtless expendi-

Shopping under the electric lights of the newly refurbished grocery business, Underhill and Son, at No. 7 High Street in 1901. These premises were to become the Oxford branch of J. Sainsbury later in the decade.

ture at the beginning of the Vacation, and debt and difficulties at the close of it.'[29] For many others, there was no such alternative and the desperate struggle for existence was marked at Magdalen Bridge in June 1898 by the presence of two pavement artists, a pavement mathematician and crippled purveyors of laces, nuts and matches.[30] The streets were filled with hawkers of goods and in April 1862, Martha Mildmay complained that

One rings to know if you want a night cap; another, whether you want laces for your ——; another, needles and knitting pins; another for crockery or glass ware; another for matches, tin ware, or tracts; and one rings and leaves a paper 'to be called for'. Then he rings again, and if the said paper cannot be found, he abuses you for losing that for which you never asked, and never wanted! [31]

Two little girls gaze in wonder as the Cowley Road sculptor Samuel Grafton puts the finishing touches to a statue of Queen Victoria in June 1897.

Children were a crucial part of a subsistence economy as these entries from the Summertown School log book record:

1865 June 14.

Emma Green and Mary Irons again away from school, the former gone to the Crescent (as a servant) and the latter gone to gather snails for the pig.

1866 February 19.

John Bunce is again absent from school. On enquiring his father says it is a case of necessity as he cannot afford to pay a man to blow the bellows in his workshop.

March 6.

An (sic) Savings has leave to be absent from school in order to go to work in the fields. His parents say that his father's wages are small and that he must now get help to support himself.

October 15.

Small School this morning. The bulk of the absent children are assisting their parents in getting in the potatoes.[32]

In the worst weather Oxford became ' a starvation town' and over 1,700 men were out of work in January 1879.[33] Relief work was sometimes found for the unemployed and in the early 1860s for instance, Willow Walks to the south and east of Port Meadow were created, largely at the expense of Richard Greswell of Worcester College.[34] In January 1882, a Committee was formed to alleviate distress in the city, distributing soup to the poor and organizing the repair of paths around Port Meadow.[35]

In these circumstances and in a city dominated by small employers, labour had very little bargaining power. Two hundred men applied for twenty labourers' jobs in January 1871, declaring that they were ready to work for the lowest wage that would enable them to obtain food for themselves and their families.[36] Builders' labourers went on strike for an extra 6d. a week in May 1867, but their employers refused to negotiate and simply took on other men 'as there is no shortage of labourers'. [37] In May 1896, about sixty machine boys at the University Press struck for higher wages, but this dispute lasted only 24 hours. The OXFORD CHRONICLE reported that:

The Authorities at the Press never consider any application for an increase in wages which is made under pressure and on Friday morning most of the boys were re-admitted at the same wages as before. The ringleaders of the demonstration, however, were told that as they had absented themselves from work they need not return.[38]

Employees of the St Giles' Brickworks in Woodstock Road in the 1890s. One of several brickworks around the city, this one was established in 1872 and was run by Edward Webb for many years from 1887.

Looking after the horses at the Randolph Hotel stables in about 1900. With so much horse-drawn traffic, many men and boys found work in stable yards off busy central streets.

AMERICANS IN OXFORD.

1st American—'Do you reckon this car will put us down at the famous Oxford University?'

2nd American—'Hustle round Ma, our train leaves for Stratford in 30 minutes.'

Tourists in a desperate hurry to see Oxford in the 1900s. Increased travel by train and steamship made tourism a new source of prosperity although the visitors often became the butt of jokes like this.

With the growth of the railway network and international travel, attracting more visitors to Oxford seemed to offer one way of improving the city's prosperity; as J. T. Dodd wrote in 1898:

If strangers only realised what a pleasant place Oxford is in the summer, I feel sure that many would spend their summer holidays here.[39]

The first Oxford Extension students came to stay at Oxford during the Long Vacation of 1888 and a city tourist committee was attracting large parties of visitors to Oxford by the late 1890s.[40] International tourism was increasing and Edward Thomas described an undergraduate trying to fool an American tourist into believing that the Examination Schools were the Martyrs' Memorial and the examinees the martyrs:

'But I thought they were burned three hundred years ago?'

'Sir', said the undergraduate impressively, 'they are martyred twice daily.'

'Well, I guess Oxford is very Middle Age and all that, but I didn't know it went so far as that': and the humane visitor went away, talking of agitation in the *New York Herald*.[41]

In the Long Vacation of 1900, Barbara Burke commented on

another familiar feature of Oxford life, an Oxford Guide. He was taking round a party of eager tourists. They had just bestowed a hurried five minutes on the Bodleian, and were in full flight to see the spot on which Cranmer, Latimer and Ridley gave their bodies to be burned. We listened for a while to the informing discourse of the guide and to the 'Ach! so' of the German and the 'Say! were they burned right here?' of the American part of his clients. Brownie's countrymen contributed the 'Oh, really!' of the touring Briton. Three Japanese gentlemen, very small and grave and neat, all armed with Baedekers, gave a cosmopolitan touch to the group.[42]

W.R. Morris and his family in the 1890s. At this time, Morris still ran a small bicycle business behind his home in James Street; within a few years, he was to bring major industry to an unsuspecting city.

In January 1890, A.W. Hall identified a 'large industry for Oxford' as the best solution to chronic underemployment.[43] At the time, there must have seemed little prospect of this but, in 1893, W.R. Morris began to make bicycles at the back of his father's house at No. 16 James Street. In September 1899,[44] he announced the opening of new premises at:

48a High Street, (opposite the New Examination Schools). Where your orders, &c., will receive prompt attention.

DON'T FAIL TO SEE THE
£10 – 10 – 0 'MORRIS'

BUILT TO ORDER & FULLY GUARANTEED.
ALSO THE
'MORRIS' TANDEM FOR TWO LADIES.
MY OWN DESIGN

Within a very few years, Morris was to become one of Britain's largest motor manufacturers and Oxford an industrialized city.

Castle Street in 1913 when gabled and timber-framed buildings still seemed to line the rise towards Queen Street. In fact, Shuffrey's chosen viewpoint carefully masked the red-brick Salvation Army Citadel which had been built beyond the newsagent's in 1888.

Turl Street and All Saints' church in 1912. Two well-known Oxford shops — Walters' the tailors and the bespoke shoemakers Ducker's — were established in the Turl in the late nineteenth century, but J.A. Shuffrey's watercolour shows how little the appearance of the street had changed during Victorian's reign.

Bible Stall at St Giles' Fair in the 1890s. The bookstall was an annual feature for many years, imparting a solemn message to passing fair-goers. The boy on the right with the feather brush introduces a mischievous element and it was not unknown for his elders to overturn the stall.

CHAPTER EIGHT

Church and School

Early Victorian Oxford was embroiled in a religious controversy fuelled by the adherents of the Oxford Movement, the so-called Tractarians or Puseyites. Their objective of returning the Anglican communion to a 'Catholic', but not Roman Catholic, Church excited fierce passions and one of the movement's leading figures, E.B. Pusey, was said to punish his children by holding their fingers to a lighted candle as a foretaste of hell-fire. On one occasion, a garrulous lady on the horse-bus between Oxford and Steventon station

Talked to him of the Newmanites and of Dr Pusey, adding that the latter, she was credibly informed, sacrificed a lamb every Friday. 'I thought I ought to tell her,' he said; 'so I answered, "My dear madam, I am Dr Pusey, and I do not know how to kill a lamb."'[1]

In 1843, Pusey was suspended from preaching before the University for two years and, in the same year, J.H. Newman resigned the vicarage of St Mary the Virgin church, retiring to Littlemore and becoming a Roman Catholic in October 1845. Others followed suit, but Pusey and John Keble remained staunchly Anglican. Much of the controversy was spent and James Pycroft remarked that, 'A little later, going to Rome created as little public interest as going to Romford.'[2] According to G.V. Cox, Oxford conversation turned to railways:

Instead of High Church, Low Church, or Broad Church, they talked of high embankments, the broad gauge, and low divi-

dends: Brunel and Stevenson were in men's mouths instead of Dr Pusey or Mr Golightly; Mr Hudson was in the ascendant instead of Dr Faussett; and speculative theology gave way to speculations in railroad shares.[3]

The Oxford Movement lived on, particularly in Oxford, through its attempts to re-invigorate the Church at parochial level. Revd Thomas Chamberlain, the vicar of St Thomas's, surprised congregations in December 1846 by having much of the service sung or chanted;[4] W.E. Sherwood recalled that the church

was terribly in advance of the times, and had vestments, and altar lights, and Sisters of Mercy, and all sorts of strange horrors which were utterly anathema to an old-fashioned churchman like my father, so that we were strictly forbidden to put so much as our noses inside it.[5]

The High Church tradition reached a peak at St Barnabas', a new church built in Jericho at the expense of Thomas Combe, superintendent of the University Press. The building was consecrated by Samuel Wilberforce, Bishop of Oxford, on 19 October, 1869 after the choir, preceded by a processional cross, had marched down Cardigan Street singing 'Onward Christian Soldiers'. One mother recalled:

Our Tommy's hair had been washed and curled 'special' the day before, because he was to wear a sort of white nightgown and carry a boat! 'Boat boy'. That's what he was called. He had some incense in it you know. He was in the choir of St Paul's and the people looking on at the procession said he looked like a little angel.[6]

The new splendour of these church services with music, singing and ritual had great visual and spiritual appeal and St Barnabas' attracted large congregations, including many undergraduates. At the same time, others were repelled and in 1877, 'An English Churchman' complained that the Whitsun Service at St Barnabas' had been like a pleasure fair or a club feast:

The performance mainly consisted of a procession of men and boys in strange attire, bearing banners with curious devices, preceded by a youth tossing up and down a large pot of incense. They proceeded round and round the church singing hymns. A figure arrayed in red and yellow from head to foot, without any white (although it was Whit Sunday), was an extraordinary feature in the exhibition. Some persons may have admired him. Others must have thought him a species of guy. The rev gentleman will be more flattered if I compare him to a certain person in a wax-work show.[7]

The correspondence columns of the OXFORD CHRONICLE were regularly occupied by objections to Romish confessionals, Papist piscinas, separation of the sexes during services and 'worshippers of crosses and gee-gaws, and vestments and bread and wine.'[8] In October 1868, 'A Looker-On' saw members of the Society of St John the Evangelist, or Cowley Fathers, go into the Iron Church in Stockmore Street: 'Fancy a man wearing a petticoat, and on a wet day holding it up just the same as old Mother Gamp holds up hers.'[9]

In the 1850s and '60s, Evangelicals within the Anglican Church fought back and they acquired the patronage of several Oxford parishes, notably perhaps St Aldate's where Canon Christopher was rector from 1859 to 1905. Christopher worked tirelessly for both Town and Gown, holding services for working people in the Town Hall and

undergraduates' prayer meetings at the rectory. A lonely freshman attended one of the latter in October 1878:

As I entered, the hymn was being sung, 'How Sweet the Name of Jesus sounds in a believer's ear', and I felt I had found home. From that day, the sympathy, the advice, the hospitality, the prayers and the life of Canon Christopher helped me more than I could or ever can say.[10]

The Evangelical Alliance held a conference at Oxford in 1877 and the OXFORD TIMES felt that this had

purified the atmosphere, and . . . that Oxford is once more the site where the Bishops suffered martyrdom, where the candle was lighted by good old Latimer, which by God's grace shall not be put out in this realm of England and not a propaganda where fledgling curates, who delight in calling themselves priests, parade the streets in Romish garments.[11]

Nevertheless, Christopher reflected in 1897 that

Oxford is, on the whole, a thoroughly High Church place. Most of the well-to-do people in Oxford are High Church, if they are church people at all.[12]

The strength of this tradition had been illustrated in 1868 by the foundation of Keble College as a memorial to John Keble, a central figure in the Oxford Movement. The college was committed to High Church principles and to simple, economic living — so much so that during Lent one hungry undergraduate was summoned to the presence of the Warden, Professor Lock:

Mr Cholmely Jones, in this college we provide at breakfast, *fish* for those gentlemen who desire to fast; *cold meat* for those who would like to fast, but do not feel quite equal to it; and *hot meat* for those who wish to do nothing at all in that way. I

The Cowley Fathers leaving their Mission House in Marston Street to attend the dedication of St John the Evangelist church on 12 May 1896. Founded in 1866, they established missions throughout the world and were also an active force in local parish work.

observed this morning, Mr Cholmely Jones, that you partook of all three.[13]

The struggle between High and Low Church was paralleled by theological differences between Anglicans and Nonconformists. In 1877, for example, Revd W. Black, one of the Cowley Fathers, argued that worship outside the Church was really devil worship:

The Church is Christ, and all who separate themselves from the Church go from Christ, and are in the devil. . . . When I said you worshipped the devil when you worship what you call Christ in a Dissenter's chapel, I said what is quite true. . . . All that is outside of Him, whether we call it good or bad, is of the devil.[14]

In June 1888, the editor of the Cowley Road Congregational church magazine LIGHT AND LOVE warned against the ritualistic teaching of Anglican clergymen

which feeds the church of Rome, and utterly subverts the Gospel of our Lord Jesus Christ, by putting ceremonial observance in place of faith in Christ as the one essential condition of salvation and spiritual life.[15]

This inter-denominational rivalry seemed at times to assume as much importance as the need for missionary endeavour and, in 1898, members of the church choir at Summertown were 'locked out' after refusing the new vicar's order to stay out of 'a dissenting place of worship'.[16] By this time, however, there were signs of a more ecumenical spirit, particularly between Low Church Anglicans and Nonconformists, and, in May 1898, the mayor, Cllr. G.W. Cooper, and twenty-nine councillors attended the first civic service at a Nonconformist place of worship, the New Road Baptist church.[17]
The various denominations in Victorian Oxford made sterling efforts to carry their civilizing mission to 'people that lived regardless of God and his holy day.'[18] In 1865, Sunday evening services for the destitute in St Ebbe's were said to have reclaimed many people:

Whitsuntide procession through the streets of Jericho led by the choir of St Barnabas' in about 1900. To the High Churchman, this practice brought the Church out into the community; to the Low Churchman or the Nonconformist, it smacked of Popery.

Drunkards, wife-beaters, who have not gone to any worship for 10 or 20 years, now enjoy the services and lead a new life.[19]

The Oxford evangelist, Henry Bazely, preached in the courts and alleys of St Aldate's parish and, from 1870, at the Martyrs' Memorial on Sunday evenings. Here, he faced regular disruption from undergraduates and on one occasion in 1878 or 1879, they tried to interrupt the service in a novel way:

They had strewn gunpowder in and about the crowd, and more thickly round Bazely himself. At a signal lighted fusees were let fall on the ground, and at the explosion the crowd darted back in alarm. He himself remained unmoved; he went on preaching as if he neither saw nor heard what was passing.

Castle Street and the Salvation Army Citadel in about 1900. The building of the citadel in 1888 followed seven hectic years of missionary work in the poorer areas of the city.

In a few moments the people, seeing his calm demeanour, gathered quietly about him as attentive as before.[20]

Evangelizing received a new impetus in the 1880s as the popularizing work of the Salvation Army was countered by an Anglican Church Army. These evangelists ignored considerable personal risks and, in October 1881 for example, Captain Winzar led a Salvation Army procession through huge crowds in St Aldate's:

the surging crowd, the weird strains of the singing, the noise and shouting, were simply indescribable; striving against numbers the Army managed to reach the entrance to Speedwell Street, when 'Captain' Winzar was collared and thrown amid exulting cries; and then ensued a general stampede, the Army deserting their leader, and seeking refuge in alleys and lanes, and even in public and private houses. 'The Captain' fortunately managed to free himself for a while, and wended his way up St Aldate's Street, until he reached Brewer Street, when he was again thrown, and again, for the third time, near Pembroke Street, after which, escorted by some constables, he managed to reach the Police Station, where he remained under protection, apart from the fear of 'Judge Lynch', for above an hour, when, the tumult having subsided, he departed – not to the barracks – but home, happy to escape.[21]

In the early 1880s, Frank Webster's St Aldate's Church Salvation Army boldly decided to hold an open-air meeting at St Giles' Fair. The crowd gave them a lively reception:

The Principal's coat was torn, our tunics were soon in pieces, and our caps were treated like footballs. They spat in our faces, bad eggs were thrown and all kinds of refuse hurled at us, but by God's grace we were enabled to hold on.[22]

The inter-denominational struggle for souls was repeated in the field of education, traditionally a religious preserve. Seeking funds for 'a better sort of school' in Osney in 1874, the vicar of

Children emerging from the Boatmen's Floating Chapel near Hythe Bridge in 1851. The chapel, designed by J.M. Derick and funded by the Oxford coal merchant, Henry Ward, was built for canal boatmen and their families in 1839. It was used for church services on Sundays and as a school during the week.

St Frideswide's, Revd G.L. Kemp, therefore laid stress on the fact that many boys

have been drawn to the Wesleyan or Central Elementary schools in Oxford – mostly though, to the Wesleyan. By this means dissent is much strengthened amongst a class of persons socially predisposed to those principles – e.g. *school treats* are attended by parents as well as children in many instances. Day school usually involves Sunday school – and that again the dissenting chapel for both parents and children. *Missionary* interest is excited in favour of the Wesleyan Missionary Society and in these and many other ways much ground is lost to the Church.[23]

In these circumstances public education was seen as a kind of trench warfare in which Anglicans and the supporters of Nonconformist or undenominational schooling fought for tactical supremacy. In Osney and Summertown, for example, Baptist schools rivalled the parish

Girls at St Mary and St John School in East Oxford in 1897. The school was built in 1895 with substantial financial assistance from the Cowley Fathers in a desperate bid to keep 'Godless' board schools out of this fast-growing area.

City of Oxford High School for Boys in 1901. The school was opened in 1881 to give Oxford boys the chance of a university education. This group includes one of the school's most famous pupils, T.E. Lawrence, who is standing towards the back in a distinctive striped jumper.

schools and, in Cowley St John, an East Oxford British School was opened in 1882 to provide an alternative to the High Church schools run by the Revd R.M. Benson.[24] Anglicans fearing the introduction of 'Secular Schools' bitterly opposed moves towards establishing a School Board in 1870, but the elections in February 1871 produced a small majority 'pledged to maintain as far as possible, the existing system'.[25] With the help of wealthy sympathizers and grant aid, churchmen managed to keep the Anglican-dominated voluntary system intact until the very end of the century when the School Board was forced to re-house the Central Boys', Central Girls' and East Oxford British Schools in new board schools.[26]

Oxford's Victorian schools mirrored the social stratification of society. At the foot of the ladder were schools like Mrs James Morrell's school for female servants in St Clement's[27] or the Oxford Ragged School in St Ebbe's which was founded in 1859

for the purpose of gathering in from the streets, and instructing those of the youth of both sexes who, from the poverty, too often combined with the vice of their parents had the usual sources of education shut against them . . .[28]

The Day Industrial School established by the School Board in 1879 similarly aimed to cater for children who would not or could not go to school and for those who had perhaps

obtained such an unenviable notoriety that they could not find a school to receive them if they were willing to go. The boys would be taught some rough trade, such as rough carpentering, cobbling and gardening, and the girls would be instructed in washing, mending, cooking, etc.[29]

The public elementary schools occupied the next few rungs of the ladder, being effectively classified by the size of their fees. When the building of SS Philip and James' Boys' School was proposed in 1879, it was therefore to be of

A higher grade than the ordinary parochial schools, with a general fee of 9d. per week, – the highest recognised by the Education Department. The need of such a school may be estimated from the fact, that a great proportion of the many new houses in this parish are of the class from which its pupils would naturally be taken. There is at present no public elementary school of this grade in North Oxford.[30]

From 1891, fees were no longer compulsory but social differences were generally maintained because schools in poorer areas became free while others continued to charge. Thus, in Cowley St John, fee-paying senior schools were retained for parents 'who desire for their children Christian privileges and the teaching of the Church, and who also are unwilling to send them amongst the promiscuous surroundings of an entirely free school.'[31]

The city's 'Ladder of Learning' was completed in 1881 with the foundation of the City of Oxford High School for Boys, a grammar school for boys resident in Oxford which set out to prepare them for a university education.[32] In North Oxford, however, an alternative educational ladder was being provided by the preparatory schools Summer Fields, founded in 1864, and the Dragon School (founded in 1877) and by the public school St Edward's (founded 1863).[33] Girls of the same class were provided for at the Oxford High School for Girls founded in 1875 by the Girls' Public Day School Trust. This school moved to purpose-built premises in Banbury Road in 1880 and with fees ranging from 9 to 15 guineas a year was open to girls 'from all walks of life'.[34] In truth, this meant only the uneasy co-existence between academics' daughters and those of successful townsfolk; the fees were more than sufficient to exclude all others.

A temporary electric lamp-post at Carfax in 1892. The Oxford Electric Co. began to supply electricity from its works in Osney on 18 June 1892, but the arrival of ornamental lamp columns from Germany was delayed. Wooden poles were a last-minute expedient.

CHAPTER NINE

Public Services

*I*n *early Victorian Oxford, as in other contemporary towns and cities, basic utilities were few and those that existed were generally inadequate or unequally shared. The corporation, for example, managed a waterworks which pumped water direct from the River Thames, but the plant was*

so constructed at Folly Bridge (as if the very name was contagious), that whenever the river was overflowed (and that happens, as we all know, pretty often in autumn, winter, and spring) no water could be supplied to the town![1]

In 1848, Oxford could only give the most unsatisfactory answers to questions posed by the Health of Towns' Association:

What is the present sanatory state of the town of Oxford?
— So defective as to demand immediate alteration.
Have the authorities of the town suggested spontaneously the adoption of complete sanatory arrangements of any one kind; for example, complete drainage, that is, complete house drainage, with sewerage and with suburban drainage?
— Neither; and the greatest unwillingness exists in the Board of Commissioners to be driven into expenses for sanatory purposes.
Have the authorities of the town given any indication of their knowledge of the kind and degree of influence which the condition of the suburban districts exercises over the health of the town?

— Certainly not.
Have the authorities of the town done anything to obtain an abundant and economical supply of water; and are they aware of the advantages of the constant over the intermittent supply?
— The water supplied by the Corporation is intermittent and very deficient. They are in the lowest level of the city, and at the tail of nearly all the sewers! Beautiful water, and to an unlimited extent, might be obtained at a much higher level at about a mile from the city. Out of 4,500, only 160 take the water, caused by the irregular and deficient supply, and the high price charged for it.
Have the authorities of the town made any exertions to obtain a combination of these works – that is, the water supply with the sewerage, the house drainage, the street cleaning, and the protection of property and life from fire.
— Never; and not likely to do so, till compelled by Parliamentary interposition.
If they have in no instance effected this combination of works, have they done any one of these things separately well?
— Neither. The culvertage has been done without system, and only in the principal streets. The house drainage is infamous, and checked by a silly regulation of the Commissioners, which requires that every house-drain shall have a grating at the opening into the culvert, with bars only three-quarters of an inch apart, thereby throwing back upon the dwelling-house all that is noxious and offensive.

Were any of the existing defects in the sewerage, drainage, and supply of water ever pointed out by the local authorities, before attention was directed to them by someone not belonging to their body?

— The defects have often been pointed out in the management; the 'let alone' system prevails, and nothing but the interference of the Government will change it.[2]

The city's various local authorities were generally noted for a laissez-faire *attitude and for their parsimony. In 1836, Edward Latimer, an Oxford wine-merchant, lambasted the Market Committee for procrastinating and constantly changing its mind over plans to redevelop the Covered Market:*

Public Works are carried on with Spirit, Energy, Liberality and on a scale of Magnificence which does credit to the parties, in every town in England but Oxford, but this famed city which ought to be an example to all the Kingdom, is notorious for having its public works executed upon a stingy, narrow minded diminutive contemtible (sic) scale . . .[3]

William Sherwood recalled the city's roads and primitive street-watering methods in the 1860s:

The main roads were pitched with kidney pebbles. . . . In the High Street there was also a strip of granite setts all down the centre of the road. The watering of the High was done by a very primitive method. The fire plugs were opened at Carfax soon after seven o'clock in the morning, and, as the water ran down the gutters, two men went with boards to which some kind of sacking or coarse material was attached, and with these they dammed the gutters at intervals and threw water with wooden shovels across the road, passing gradually down the street until they came to Magdalen, and doing their work very thoroughly.[4]

Away from the city centre road conditions could be appalling and,

A water cart outside Magdalen Hall, soon to become Hertford College, in 1857. Until the introduction of asphalt road surfaces, water carts were much needed in dry weather to lay the dust in city streets.

in 1877, T.H. Ward compared Banbury Road beyond Park Town with

a bog, a morass, a great dismal swamp. In places it was one level pool of soft and soup-like mud; in places it was seamed with a hundred ridges of crisp and crusty consistency; here were ruts, half-a-foot deep; there were mighty hollows into which the rain water had trickled till the pools were as the pools on the sea-shore. A train of covered spring-carts, coming from the Oxford market, passed me at a trot, it was like artillery-waggons dashing across a ford. At one point a country woman, bracing herself for a serious effort, managed to cross; she emerged bespattered to her knees.[5]

Deplorable as these conditions were in daylight, muddy roads and uneven footways became much more dangerous at night when 'persons are obliged to grope through them in the dark.' In 1851, a report stressed that, in Jericho for example, there were too few street lamps and that the supply of gas was neither constant nor liberal. Furthermore, there were complaints in all suburban areas about the practice of not lighting the street lamps when the moon was expected:

It may, and often does, happen, that on particular nights, when the moon, according to the indications of the almanack, is expected to be high in the heavens, the weather proves rainy and murky in the extreme, and the light wholly obscured by clouds. The consequence is, that the public are often deprived of the light of the lamps on nights when it is really most needed. . . .[6]

During Victoria's reign, legislation, public pressure and civic pride combined with technological developments to make changes in all these areas. In 1856, the corporation opened a new city waterworks at New Hinksey, utilizing the excavated Railway Lake as a reservoir. By 1867, city water was supplied to nearly half of the houses in the Local Board district, and the Board's Inspector of Nuisances gradually compelled owners to provide a proper supply to older properties. Nevertheless the supply remained intermittent, eliciting this complaint from an East Oxford resident during the cholera epidemic in 1866:

The Iffley-road, the Cowley-road, and the Headington-road have become powerful off-springs of the good old City of Oxford. Those parts abound with industrious and well-disposed people, with large families. What have these people done that they at this moment are in imminent danger to be swept away by cholera? For there you will find water-closets in the houses which, for the last week, have had no other water supply but what the people may have poured down.[7]

It was not until 1877 that the building of a high-level reservoir at the top of Headington Hill ensured a continuous supply in all areas of

the city. The long-suffering consulting engineer, Thomas Hawksley, sought to justify the delay:

It was a city of learning, and they took their tone from the learned men; they took a very much longer time to settle a great question. Under these circumstances, although he had been a little of a victim to that habit, what they had been performing justified them in taking a quarter of a century in considering in what way they should improve their waterworks. The time had not been thrown away. When he was called in to give his advice the idea which presented itself was that they should inaugurate a work which would not have been of one-fourth the value which after twenty-five years they had been able to carry out. The ideas they had then would now have become futile, if they had not remained a longer time to think upon this subject, and come in the end to a perfectly right conclusion.[8]

Even after this the city water was still unfiltered and, in February 1880, Henry Taunt challenged the mayor to prove that it was fit to drink:

Is the Mayor aware of the fact that when the steam fire engine was tried on Carfax it came to a stop, and the firemen had to clear their valves, &c., from the mussels before they could go on; that over two bushels of mussels were turned out on Carfax at the time?

Is the Mayor aware of the fact that City water will, if exposed to the sun, give off a most unpleasant rotten smell in one summer day?

Did he ever hear of the fact that in less than three hours, when running the City water from my tap through muslin, I caught 37 fresh water shrimps supplied with the water, and which were afterwards exhibited in the Town Hall, some being enlarged by the oxyhydrogen microscope?![9]

The corporation was persuaded to construct filter beds at the waterworks in 1883 and, four years later, pipes were laid from the Thames

The bringers of main drainage to Oxford in 1876. William H. White, the city engineer, is the bearded man sitting in the second row with his assistant engineer, E.S. Cobbold, to his right; in front of them, G.T. Acock was the contractor for much of the work.

Navvies forming the new cut of the River Cherwell, an important flood prevention scheme in 1884 which provided an outfall for the river near Long Bridges. In the background, Iffley Road had, from the 1850s, been lined by villas which offered extensive views across the Thames Valley.

Workmen washing sand for the filter beds at the Oxford Waterworks in September 1911. The waterworks were transferred from Folly Bridge to New Hinksey in 1856, but the city's water supply was unfiltered until 1883.

at King's Weir above Oxford to the Railway Lake, promising an adequate supply, 'not only for the benefit of the present generation, but to those who came after them. . . .'[10]

With its sewerage as with its water supply, Oxford was slow to resolve problems that were plainly stated in the 1851 sanitary report. Giving evidence at the enquiry, the surgeon Thomas Allen stated:

Throughout Oxford cess-pools are not only general, but almost universal. Some parts of St Ebbe's might be described as a swamp converted into a cess-pool; these sometimes burst and flood the yards with liquid filth. . . . The privies are too few, and too filthy for any decent community.[11]

In 1851, Cubitt and Smith suggested the building of a main sewer conveying town sewage to open reservoirs below Kennington.[12] The Paving Commissioners did not act on this recommendation, however, and handed the problem on to their successor authority, the Oxford Local Board, in 1864. Faced with conflicting professional advice, the Local Board agreed in principle to accept the 'separate' system, excluding rainfall from the sewers.[13] By 1872, it was 'weary of the inaction and timidity which have so long characterized its movements upon this important question', and internal drainage works began the following year. At the last minute residents in Iffley mounted a campaign against the proposed siting of the outfall sewer:

Iffley consists mainly of valuable villa property, owned or occupied by gentlemen who have been induced to settle there by the salubrity and picturesqueness of the situation, and the neighbourhood of the unique old Church. . . . They believe that if such plan be carried out it will be injurious in many ways to the inhabitants of Iffley, not only by the temporary annoyance which will be caused in bringing the works through a line of gardens and pleasure grounds, but by the permanent discomfort and injury to health which they believe will ensue.

That even if such discomfort and injury shall not be the consequence, yet the very fact of the drainage works being established here, and irrigation carried on in the vicinity, will lead to a serious deterioration of property. Already persons seeking for houses have declined to take one at Iffley, and some of the gentry have declared their intention to leave the place.[14]

Nevertheless their fears were dismissed and the drainage scheme went ahead at a cost of over £180,000, putting Oxford into the van of sanitary progress. In 1878, the city's Medical Officer of Health reported:

The main drainage of Oxford is now, so far as Oxford and its immediate surroundings are concerned, in full working order, the sewage being carried away by it to a distant point, and there disposed of by a temporary outlet into the river. In the course of the year a great number of foul privies have been abolished, and w.c.s substituted for them, but owing to the very great number there were to be dealt with, a good deal in this direction still remains to be done. It will be seen from the report of the Inspector of Nuisances that as many as 870 privies were thus converted, and as in most of these cases a supply of city water for domestic purposes was obtained, it is evident that very substantial progress in sanitary matters has been made.[15]

Fire-fighting, as well as water supply and drainage, featured among the questions asked by the Health of Towns' Association in 1848. At this time, however, the city lacked any form of fire-fighting organization and in 1854, the city's fire-engine was sold because it was out of repair.[16] Desultory negotiations between the various Oxford local authorities achieved nothing, and indignant residents formed an Oxford Volunteer Fire Brigade after a serious fire in St Aldate's in June 1870 which claimed two lives.[17] The new force acquired a steam fire-engine but the Oxford Local Board, disapproving of this voluntary body, arranged for the city police to become an official fire brigade using old engines supplied by the University. The result was often farce of the richest kind as the police, often the first to hear of a fire, hastened to the scene, either failing to alert the volunteers at all or waiting until their own engine was on its way.[18] The rivalry reached a climax in October 1886 during a fire at the Cowley Fathers' Mission House in Marston Street:

The police were early on the spot with the Local Board engine, and at this time the wing of the building where the fire was located was a mass of flames, and fears were expressed as to the safety of the adjoining property. A second plug was drawn and, being a small main, the members in charge of the hose belonging to the Brigade found themselves deprived of

Christmas greetings from members of the Oxford Volunteer Fire Brigade in 1893. The Central Fire Station in New Inn Hall Street opened in 1874 and, in 1878, it became one of the first buildings in Oxford to be linked to the telephone.

anything like an adequate supply of water. This gave rise to some words, and matters were not improved by the Waterworks turncock putting in the fire plug, and thus stopping work. It is needless to say that whilst the dispute was proceeding valuable time was being lost, and the fire making headway. A large crowd had collected, and far from complimentary remarks were applied to both the brigade and the police.[19]

After this fiasco, it was at last agreed that the police would concentrate on preserving life and maintaining order, leaving the task of fire-fighting to the brigade.[20]

By comparison with life-threatening issues, problems relating to road maintenance, street-lighting and refuse disposal could be seen as trivial, and individual or community protest played an important part

The aftermath of a serious fire on the corner of St Aldate's and Pembroke Street in June 1870. Two lives were lost in the fire which exposed the utter inadequacy of fire-fighting arrangements in Oxford and led to the formation of the Oxford Volunteer Fire Brigade.

in resolving them. In January 1865, for example, the first three residents of Norham Gardens, Goldwin Smith, Montagu Burrows and William Phillips, petitioned the Paving Commissioners, 'having suffered much inconvenience for want of light thro' (sic) these winter nights'; in February, the commissioners agreed to light their darkness with a single lamp.[21] *'Ratepayer' in East Oxford chose to make his grievance public by writing to the* OXFORD CHRONICLE *in May 1866:*

Since that part of Cowley came under the Local Board, we have been expecting great reformation, but still we are going on in the same old style. Certainly, we got a few lamp posts stuck up, but the lights are so bad, and the posts so far apart, that standing near one (on a dark night), you cannot see the other, and more accidents have occurred since they were put up than before. . . .

And now we have so much dust, the overlooker has been spoken to, but no change for the better. The water cart comes along the road once a day, generally about 12 or 1 o'clock, and at such a pace that he gets over the ground with two or three barrels. Were he to do it properly, it would require six or seven.

Now, Mr Editor, is it right that the contractor should scamp his work like this, and is it right that the Local Board should simply sit to make rates, and we still remain in dirt, dust, and darkness?[22]

In poorer areas, people were less ready to complain for fear of offending their landlords or because they did not expect their protests to be heard. No lighting was therefore provided in the passageway leading to York Place, St Clement's, until 1897 when a benevolent North Oxford landlady, Agnes Weld, wrote to the mayor insisting that it was essential:

When taking Christmas gifts to my tenants I had to grope my way along and I am sure that the immorality which has been such a trial to me in the case of more than one of my tenants

is largely owing to that passage being one of the dark places of the earth. . . .'[23]

With refuse collection and disposal too, conditions tended to improve more strikingly in the most influential neighbourhoods. Thus, in 1891, an East Ward ratepayer drew attention to

The filthy condition of our streets, caused by the householders bringing out the house refuse and emptying it into the road, thus exposing the lighter portion, such as paper, &c., to blow about all over the place. . . . At times I have known it between 3 and 4 in the afternoon before the carts have come round to collect the rubbish. Even at the time I write pieces of paper are being blown about Regent Street, which have been there since Saturday last; there is also an old tin bucket, which the boys have been kicking about, thus making a most awful noise. . . .

I fail to understand why the North Ward should have so much attention shown to it; one never sees unsightly deposits there. The men with the carts go to the houses and carry the refuse direct to the carts, and the dirt-boxes or bins, as the case may be, are then returned to the houses. . . . I do not know whether the Sanitary Committee have given the men instructions to carry out what I have mentioned above with respect to the North Ward, or whether the men do it for their own benefit; if the latter be the case, I don't blame them; but, as far as I know, the working classes of the East, West, and South Wards would be quite as ready to give a small present at the time which will soon be here now as their neighbours in the north of Oxford, if the same attention were shown them. . . .[24]

The dumping of street and household refuse was a very haphazard affair and, in 1867, there was a complaint from Jericho that low-lying fields beyond Cranham Street

have been considered fit receptacles of all kinds of refuse, vegetables, putrid fish, dead rats, and other animals; and this practice

A horse tram at the Kingston Road terminus in about 1890. Many people welcomed the arrival of trams in 1881 but others viewed their presence in historic Oxford streets as a hideous anachronism.

of emptying not merely harmless rubbish but decaying and decomposing matter of every kind upon these grounds, in immediate proximity to inhabited dwellings, is still continued. . . . The stench arising from these heaps of various kinds of filth is most offensive and intolerable, and calculated to produce fevers and other infectious diseases, especially as the weather is now becoming milder, and the sun increasing in power. Surely the health of one portion of the community is as valuable as that of another portion, and has equal claims to public protection; and I should wish to inquire by whose authority this is done, and whether it is legal and according to existing sanitary regulations, that, close to dwelling-houses and barely half-a-mile from the central parts of the town, garbage, animal and vegetable, should be deposited, there to lie uncovered in large quantities.

I would ask whether this state of things would be allowed to take place in Merton fields or in Christ Church meadows? Is the law to be interpreted, one way for the rich and another way for the poor? [25]

Nine years later, however, land to the north of Cranham Street was being similarly treated although it was already probable that Juxon Street would be extended across it. By contrast, rubbish dumping in old gravel diggings in Norham Road soon stopped after a local resident, Miss Sawbridge, complained, in June 1879:

Whilst I write, the Local Board men are emptying their cart of rubbish in front of this house. . . . Lately the women dust-pickers have brought their donkey-carts and turned out the *refuse* of their pickings – and this morning the *road* was strewn with every imaginable dirty *papers* (sic) you can think of. . . . [26]

In some respects, however, even the influential were not able to stem the tide of progress that seemed to threaten Oxford's very character. Horse trams began to run on 1 December 1881, welcomed by some as 'a great convenience to the labouring and working classes'; others saw them a refuge from

Parties of roughs . . . who blow their beery breath and foul tobacco smoke, accompanied by still fouler expressions, into the face of every woman and girl who is not accompanied by a protector strong enough to avenge the insult. [27]

To a substantial minority, these benefits were more than outweighed by the aesthetic affront to 'the matchless symmetry of Oxford streets'. 'B' in the OXFORD UNDERGRADUATE'S JOURNAL *wrote:*

Trams we will not forgive, we can't abide 'em
To Coventry with any man that's seen inside 'em
Yet 'tis no good; they mind not what we say
And every tram, you know, must have its *way*.
Then how to express our useless indignation
From Oaths refrain in spite of all temptation
Our pillows down our throats we're forced to cram
Since every malediction rhymes with Tram. [28]

Still more controversial was the widening of Magdalen Bridge which the tramway made necessary. A huge campaign against the proposal generated a petition signed by Tennyson, Browning, Ruskin, Holman Hunt, Burne Jones, and the architects Bodley and Street. The views of 'artistic souls' were dismissed by the Local Board in January 1882 after Dr Child argued that

The bridge bore the same relationship to the town that a pair of boots did to the wearer. The people to judge where the shoe pinched were the people who wore the shoes. It would not be a sufficient reason for keeping a growing boy in tight shoes because his maiden aunt who came from Brompton said he looked sweetly pretty in them. [29]

The bridge was subsequently widened by 20 ft on the south-west side in 1882–3, the parapet being rebuilt in facsimile.

In addition to horse trams, technological developments brought the telephone and electricity to Victorian Oxford. The arrival of the

The widening of Magdalen Bridge in progress during the winter of 1882–3. Aesthetic opinion had been much affronted by the proposal to widen this eighteenth-century bridge and change a view which was seen as quintessentially Oxford.

*telephone in January 1878 was announced by JACKSON'S
OXFORD JOURNAL which told readers that:*

When communication is desired, the operator at either end of
the wire first touches an electric stud, which causes a bell to
sound at the other end, and thus calls attention to the fact that
a message is impending. The message is spoken through a fun-
nel-shaped instrument to the listener, whose ear is applied to
one precisely similar attached to the other end of the wire.
The operator at Osney kindly talked, laughed, sang, and
whistled for our edification, and every note seemed to be
accurately conveyed to us, whilst his replies certified that we
were equally intelligible to him.[30]

*Plans were made to supply Oxford with electricity as early as
1883, but the chairman of the Local Board warned the company:*

The buildings in Oxford were very old, and as it was full of historical monuments and memorials, it was not the kind of place
to be pulled to pieces by experiments, and it would be better to
go to newer towns, and when it was agreed which was the best
way of lighting they could come and light Oxford.[31]

*Nine years later, the Oxford Electric Company opened its generat-
ing station at Cannon Wharf, Osney, a site chosen because it*

secures easy access of coal from the river and railway, abundant water for condensation, and suitable water for feed for
steam. It is in a district in which the better parts of the town
are not likely to be affected by any accompanying circumstances, such as the movement of coal or ashes and other
objectional qualities of such a works when placed in or near
the better parts of the town.[32]

The new illuminant was enthusiastically received by Hilaire Belloc:

> Descend, O Muse, from thy divine abode,
> To Osney, on the Seven Bridges Road;
> For under Osney's solitary shade
> The bulk of the Electric Light is made.
> Here are the works; – from hence the current flows
> Which (so the Company's prospectus goes)
> Can furnish to Subscribers hour by hour
> No less than sixteen thousand candle power,
> All at a thousand volts. (It is essential
> To keep the current at this high potential
> In spite of the considerable expense.)
> The Energy developed represents,
> Expressed in foot-tons, the united forces
> Of fifteen elephants and forty horses . . .[33]

*Like the early telephone, however, electricity was an expense that
few could afford. Electric lighting replaced gas in a few main streets
and was generally adopted in Oxford colleges and large business
premises. By the later 1890s the number of private consumers was
growing and, at No. 43 Banbury Road, Olwen Rhys noted in her
diary for September 1897: 'The house is becoming lively. Workmen
doing electric light to our bedroom and the walnut room. . . .' A few
days later she added, 'The electric light in our room is finished – it
looks very nice.'[34]*

*Towards the end of Victoria's reign, another new invention was
beginning to attract attention in North Oxford. In July 1900, an
observer was beginning 'to fancy that Oxford is the home of the
motor-car, and Banbury Road its peculiar exercising ground.'[35] The
mere fact that this could be so just twenty-three years after T.H. Ward
had likened the road to a great dismal swamp, was one measure of the
extent to which public services had improved.*

Oxford from North Hinksey in about 1900. Shuffrey's watercolour uses St Lawrence's church and Manor Farm as the frame to an idyllic distant view of Oxford. The development opportunities of the site led to proposals for an exclusive suburb here in the 1870s, but the scheme came to nothing.

A watercolour of George Street by E.A. Phipson in 1902. The road had become busier with traffic to and from the railway stations, but seventeenth-century houses survived beside Gloucester Street. Further down, St George's church is picked out by its weather-vane and the fire station by its tall tower.

Ramshackle housing on the south side of George Street in about 1875. These properties were demolished a few years later to make way for the City of Oxford High School for Boys.

CHAPTER TEN

Social Conditions

He only heard in part the policeman's further remarks, having fallen into thought on what struggling people like himself had stood at that Crossway, whom nobody ever thought of now. It had more history than the oldest college in the city. It was literally teeming, stratified, with the shades of human groups, who had met there for tragedy, comedy, farce; real enactments of the intensest kind. At Fourways men had stood and talked of Napoleon, the loss of America, the execution of King Charles, the burning of the Martyrs, the Crusades, the Norman Conquest, possibly of the arrival of Caesar. Here the two sexes had met for loving, hating, coupling, parting; had waited, had suffered, for each other; had triumphed over each other; cursed each other in jealousy, blessed each other in forgiveness.

He began to see that the town life was a book of humanity infinitely more palpitating, varied, and compendious than the gown life. These struggling men and women before him were the reality of Christminster, though they knew little of Christ or Minster. That was one of the humours of things. The floating population of students and teachers, who did know both in a way, were not Christminster in a local sense at all.[1]

Just a few minutes' walk from Carfax, the Crossway of Thomas Hardy's JUDE THE OBSCURE, sanitary investigators in 1851 inspected some of the crowded yards off High Street, St Thomas':

Norgrove's Yard, the next in succession on this side of the street, is one of the worst in the whole range. It is a long passage, not more than from four to five feet wide, bounded on one side by a high wall fronting the houses, which are thereby rendered close, confined, and dark. There is no drain, and the only channel for carrying off the surplus water is the gutter at the base of the wall, which is frequently overflowed, causing the fluid to run into the houses at the lower end, to the great discomfort of the inmates. The taste for flowers, which has been often found prevailing amongst the poor even amidst filth and squalor, is here curiously exemplified by one man and his wife, who have suspended against the high wall opposite their door no less than from twenty to thirty damaged kitchen utensils of various kinds, old metal pots, fenders, and crockery ware, all containing plants in luxuriant growth.[2]

In his report on the 1854 cholera epidemic at Oxford, Henry Acland wrote:

in my judgement there are few, if any, very bad dwellings in Oxford, as the civilized world has counted badness. . . . But in St Thomas's and in St Ebbe's are individual rooms and staircases whose existence is to be deplored.[3]

Better houses were to be found in newer, low-lying suburbs, but living conditions might still be atrocious. In 1872, John Venables gave evidence at the enquiry into the proposed incorporation of New Hinksey into the Oxford Local Board district:

Carfax, the busy cross-roads at the heart of the city in about 1888; a place for idle gossip and chance meetings in the shadow of St Martin's church.

Bookbinder's Yard in St Thomas's in July 1914. One of many such yards in the old city, it was approached from High Street, St Thomas's through a covered passageway.

remedy this by making four cesspools in the roadway, but they were perfectly useless, as in flood the water was always above the level of the gratings. Last winter the water stood in the road from one side to the other, and it was left in the streets till it soaked away. In the meantime the inhabitants had to enter their houses by stepping on bricks. This was worst in Cross Street, just below the schools and near to the church. They were greatly in want of some system of drainage, not only for surface water, but for slops of all kinds. Mr Venables also stated that he thought a controlling power was necessary, in as much as people were not particular what they put in the streets, and what length of time they allowed it to remain. It was not an uncommon thing for cesspools to be emptied into gardens, and the matter allowed to remain near to the dwellings. Another important thing was that the water was in danger of being contaminated by the number of cesspools which were about the place. There were 162 houses, but he could not say whether each house had a cesspool. He should imagine not. He had been obliged himself to sink three fresh wells in consequence of the water having been spoilt by the foul matter from the cesspools finding its way into them. More houses were erected every year. If they had not the sense to take care of themselves, he thought there should be some power to make them. He considered also another great blessing would arise if the Local Board came there; the children would be sent to school, which, he had no doubt, would be a great blessing to that hitherto neglected village. . . .[4]

George Arnold, the schoolmaster at New Hinksey, stated that the death rate among children there was the highest he had known; five of his pupils had died within a year.[5] Because of flooding and the condition of the roads, Osney was described in 1856 as 'only fit for the vilest demon to reside in'.[6] In late January 1873, some parts of Jericho had been flooded for more than two months and several inhabitants were forced to live upstairs. The OXFORD CHRONICLE reported that

Mr John Venables said he had had property in Hincksey for upwards of 20 years, and he had resided there five years. During the greater portion of that time the roads had been all but impossible in consequence of water standing in them, and for want of proper drainage. An attempt had been made to

'Sticky', a street seller of walking sticks, outside Oriel College in about 1900. With an uncertain and precarious income, men like this could only rent the poorest accommodation and lived in fear of the workhouse.

the ardent admirers of the well-known church of St Barnabas, on their way thither, have frequently had to wade through mud and water of a considerable depth; whilst the shopkeepers in this particular part have been unable to open and close their respective establishments without the aid of chairs. Several of the houses can only be reached by means of planks, placed from the door-steps to the centre of the road.[7]

In areas like this many residents struggled to make a living and, as Frank Collyer observed in 1893,

The honest attempt . . . to maintain a clean and well kept home, to send their children to school with neatly mended and tidy garments, and to preserve a general appearance of respectability, is very often mistaken as an indication of prosperity and comfortable circumstances, whereas it is rather a splendid tribute to the genius and thrift and untiring energy of the careful housewife.[8]

The weekly budget for one Oxford household in December 1909 shows the very low income on which a family might have to manage:

Family: Mr H a labourer, earning 12s.; Mrs H charing at 4s. a week; child, aged 2 and a half. Total income 16s.

Saturday	s.	d.
Bacon	0	3
Fish	0	2
Beef	1	1
Chops	0	4
Greens	0	2
Potatoes	0	2
Celery	0	1
Flour & Milk	0	3
Cake	0	2½
Bread & cocoa	0	6

Floods in Lake Street in about 1900. Many of the poorer nineteenth-century suburbs were built on low-lying meadows and their inhabitants suffered from regular flooding.

Monday	s.	d.
Rent	2	6
Coal	1	0
Wood	0	3½
Oil	0	4
Insurance	0	9
Bread for week, 7 2-lb. loaves	1	5½
Tuesday		
Meat scraps	0	4
Potatoes	0	1
Cheese	0	1
Wednesday		
Meat scraps	0	2
Fish	0	1
Potatoes	0	1
Thursday		
Pig pudding	0	1
Potatoes	0	1
Cheese	0	1
Friday		
Liver	0	2½
Potatoes	0	1
Milk for week	0	7
Butter	0	6
Dripping	0	3
Tea	0	6
Minding baby	1	6
Total	14	3

1s. 9d. left over for clothing, and odds and ends, such as mustard, vinegar, candles, soap, soda.[9]

A period of sickness or unemployment or simply the addition of another mouth to feed could have destroyed this precarious livelihood. Collyer, for example, described the case of

one poor fellow, a respectable and honest man, (who) was taken ill in the spring time and is only just now beginning to get to work again. He has six children, is two weeks behind with his rent, and the landlord is not a man who can afford to lose even a week's rent. . . .[10]

Misfortune could lead easily to destitution and to the need for 'Economy's' seasonable hint in December 1860:

Sir, – Will you allow me through the *Chronicle* to recommend to persons who cannot well afford an extra blanket in this cold weather, that some large sheets of brown paper, or newspapers, tacked together, and placed underneath the counterpane, will make a good substitute; also, that if four largish pebbles were sewn into the turnover of the counter pane, two at the ends, and the other two about 18 inches apart in the centre, they would make it fall closer to the back of the neck, and thus keep the wind out.[11]

Henry Acland gave a graphic account of the appalling conditions in which some people lived – and died – in 1854:

Soon after five one morning a woman awoke in the agony of cramps with intense and sudden collapse. She was seen at six. There was in her room no article of furniture but one broken chair; no bed of any kind, no fire, no food; she lay on the bare boards; a bundle of old sacking served for a pillow; she had no blanket nor any covering but the ragged cotton clothes she had on. She rolled, screaming. One woman scarcely sober sat by, with a pipe in her mouth, looking on. To treat her in this state was hopeless. She was to be removed. There was a press of work at the hospital and a delay. When the carriers came her saturated garments were stripped off, and in the finer linen and blankets of a wealthier woman she was borne away – and in the hospital she died. Her room was cleaned out: the woman that cleaned it had next night the cholera. She and her husband were drunk in bed. The agony sobered her, but her husband went reeling about the room: in a room below were smokers and drinkers. Then a woman of the streets in her gaudiness came to see her. They would not hear reason, but drank more spirits. The victim of the disease cried out to the end that her soul was everlastingly lost; and she died.[12]

Later in the Victorian period, relief agencies proliferated until,

By the later 19th century Oxford was so well provided with charitable institutions that it was scarcely possible in the poorer parts of town to be born, to give birth, to subsist or to die without coming to the notice of at least one voluntary agency.[13]

Nevertheless, these organizations tended to look askance at the feckless and 'undeserving', and, in November 1891, the city was shocked by the case of Alice Mary Hamlet, a Jericho woman, who died of starvation and neglect after giving birth to a child. Her husband was out of work, had been refused help by the Charity Organization Society and may have had too much pride to try other agencies. The inquest jury viewed the body in the bedroom where she had died:

There was no bed or bedstead, and the room was almost entirely destitute of furniture. The body was in one corner of the room, and was placed upon some straw.[14]

For the old, the poor and the unfortunate the workhouse was an ever-looming presence, threatening regulation clothing, segregation of the sexes and a 'generally monotonous existence'.[15] In August 1870, J.J. Henley, the District Poor Law inspector, was favourably impressed by the Oxford Workhouse in Cowley Road, but

He had been struck with the want of employment for the old men in the House. True, a portion of them were set to work on the grounds during the summer months; but many of these inmates might be employed in some useful work when they could not be engaged out of doors – such as cutting and bundling fagots, if the Guardians could find them a shed for the purpose. With regard to the able-bodied men, the present accommodation for them, he thought, was too comfortable – their beds were as comfortable as could well be – so that no sort of test was applied to the able-bodied men who came into the House during winter. There should be some sharper discipline if possible in order to test whether these men were really destitute; and he thought it worthy of the consideration of the Guardians whether they could not provide special wards for such a class of men, where they might be kept hard at work. They might be confined as a sort of deterrent, because the indulgences now held out to them were a kind of inducement for them to enter the House. He would also suggest that a sort of glazed canvass sheets – instead of straw – should be used as beds in the tramp wards, because then no vermin would be created in the wards. . . . To apply a proper test for the able-bodied inmates, however, they should be given just sufficient food, and no more, with plenty of labour, and fewer indulgences. Then, perhaps their numbers might be decreased and he threw out these hints for the consideration of the Guardians.[16]

The Guardians' zest for economy was seen in the use of a butcher's van to collect the body of a poor widow at New Hinksey in 1889;[17] also in their sponsored emigration of adults and children who might otherwise be a long-term burden on the rates:

EMIGRANTS FOR CANADA – Yesterday (Friday) morning a party of paupers from the Oxford Workhouse were despatched by the London and North Western Railway, *en route* for Canada. There were four single men, four young girls, and one married couple and child. Owing to the liberality of the guardians they leave with a comfortable outfit; and they

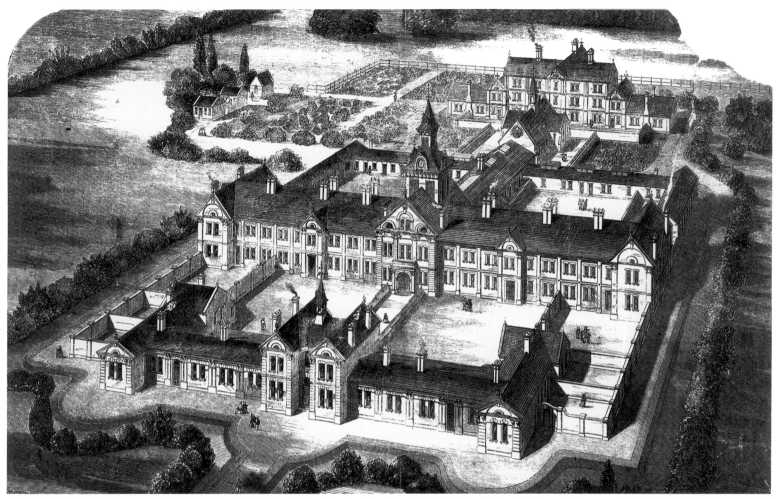

A bird's eye view of the Oxford Workhouse which opened in Cowley Road in 1864. Designed by William Fisher, an Oxford architect, it replaced an eighteenth-century building on the site of Wellington Square

seemed very cheerful in the prospect of a journey to the 'Land of the West'. The master of the workhouse has a good opinion of the party selected, and hopes by-and-bye to hear that they have achieved independence in their new home. A good many of their acquaintances were at the station to wish the emigrants farewell.[18]

Some at least of the pauper emigrants made new lives for themselves and, in May 1870, a man called Groves – 'a very troublesome fellow before he left Oxford' – wrote thanking the Guardians for their assistance and stating that he was now an industrious shoemaker in Canada.[19]

The 'troublesome fellows' who stayed behind were likely to be drawn into crime and in January 1859 for instance, Charles Hedges and James Hemmings asked the coal merchant, Ald Ward, for employment one Saturday afternoon because they had no food:

Mr Ward agreed to give them an hour's work each, for which they were to receive one shilling each, and they were employed in unloading a boat of coal. On leaving work Hedges took away with him 31 lbs of coal wrapped up in his smock frock, and was brought back with it in his possession by John Jakeman, one of Mr Ward's men, who had been apprised of it. Hemmings on leaving work was about walking off with about 14 lbs of coal, but having been observed by James Pacey, one of Mr Ward's men, who told him to put it back, he did so.[20]

Desperate circumstances might lead also to serious disturbances such as the bread riots of November 1867 when

an immense crowd, numbering about 600 or 800 men and boys, with a sprinkling of women, rushed along Cornmarket Street to the shop of Alderman Grubb, baker, amidst hooting and yelling and cries of 'We'll have our rights'. We want cheap bread'; etc. The shop was, of course, closed; but the upper windows were speedily riddled with stones and threats of firing his premises were made.[21]

Again, in September 1872 the new Licensing Act led to rioting and it was stated that:

Oxford with its libraries and precious treasures, has been for the last ten days simply at the mercy of a large mob of habitual drunkards and pothouse sots.[22]

This was the background from which the skilled artisan and the regularly employed escaped to the new and civilizing suburbs. In 1870, Joseph Eagleston praised the speculators who had promoted the growth of the city:

On the one hand there were magnificent dwellings for the

Low wages and an increase in the price of bread led to serious rioting in November 1867 when the premises of the aptly-named baker Richard Grubb were a particular target. This illustration from the Police Review *shows the attack on his shop in Cornmarket Street.*

wealthy, and quiet corners for the learned. On the other hand there were pretty little cottages, where people might remove to from the courts and alleys of the city streets and dwell in comfort and peace.[23]

According to another observer, John Abbey, in 1882,

Kingston Road is an honour to Oxford and a credit to those intelligent and industrious people who in some cases have laboured hard and long to obtain the means to purchase

Closely packed housing in the Friars district viewed from the tower of St Ebbe's church in 1908. Circus Yard in the foreground was a parking place for carriers' carts on market days and the home of Witham's tripe dressing factory.

the ground and erect such good houses with such nice gardens, just such houses as all English working men might have if they were temperate and thrifty.[24]

The new houses were not always as good as they appeared. James Walters built three Jericho houses of 'old stuff' in 1873[25] and the local historian Herbert Hurst criticized the 'unwisdom or the trickery of modern builders' who put up plaster ceilings which often cracked and fell after about four years.[26] In 1887, Edwin Gardener objected to the 4½ inch party walls between houses and 'the dreadful disagreeableness and discomfort arising from them':

There was no privacy nor quietness; their neighbours knew by the sound of their footsteps their every movement, and nothing had such a tendency to make neighbours ill friends than families living in such houses. The neighbours on either side knew every little family incident that happened in the domestic circle, such as how many times a Mrs Jones's baby cried in the night – (laughter) – or that a Mr Swiller fell on going up stairs, and afterwards received a curtain lecture (renewed laughter) – which was retailed out the next day to those living in the same street, more or less correctly. (Laughter.)[27]

With all their faults, these houses were still vastly better than dilapidated old properties in the city centre. Some rookeries were improved by the Oxford Cottage Improvement Company, founded in 1866, and others by property owners who were increasingly harassed by the work of the Nuisances Removal Officer. Many were simply demolished, however, thus reducing the stock of cheap housing. In St Thomas's, Christ Church, the major landowner, embarked on a programme of clearing older courts and erecting model lodging-houses, beginning in 1866–7 with the premises now known as Christ Church Old Buildings.[28] In June 1868, Edward Prince of Wales and the Crown Prince of Denmark visited the block which had thirty sets of dwellings on three floors.[29] Such accommodation was, of course, for 'respectable' tenants although Emma Prosser complained to Christ Church in 1875 about uninvited guests on the unlit staircase No. 2:

In consequence of *total* want of light several accidents have happened and *tramps* and dogs have taken shelter there for the night and *other annoyances* have taken place which *I* cannot name to you! One of the other tenants – the other Morng. (sic) when he went out to early work fell over a large black dog – and another stumbled over a woman who had found it convenient to *make her abode there*!![30]

The dispossessed of Victorian Oxford remained very much at the foot of the stairs while the rest of society ascended to varying levels of comfort.

A convivial gathering at The George in Botley Road in 1892. The pub remained the chief focus for popular recreation, offering not only drink and companionship but also space for a wide range of social activities.

CHAPTER ELEVEN

Popular Recreation

*F*or many Oxford residents – particularly men – recreation focused on the public house. At their most basic level, pubs offered drink and, despite the efforts of temperance organizations, there was no general reduction in the consumption of alcohol. The results of excessive drinking were all too evident and, in 1852 for example, Elijah Noon, a Jericho plasterer, was convicted of manslaughter after accidentally running his wife through with a sword during a drunken quarrel.[1] In 1862, three Summertown men had too much to drink and defied the local police constable, Thomas Hawtin, when he told them to go home quietly:

One of them turned upon him and held up his stick, and threatened to knock his b——y head off if he interrupted them. Witness seized the stick and broke it, and then the three set upon him and got him down on the ground, when he was kicked in the mouth by one of them, and his front teeth were loosened, and a quantity of blood came from his mouth on to his police cape. After he got up he used his staff, and knocked down two of the defendants with it, by which they got some severe bruises on the head.[2]

Pubs were much more than dispensaries of alcoholic drink, however, since they provided various entertainments and rooms in which local societies and groups could meet. A typical example was the Coach and Horses' (St Clement's) Piscatorial Society which, in July 1877, had its annual excursion to

one of the most out of the way dismal spots that could be selected upon the banks of the Thames. . . . From some unexplained cause but few members were present. The weather was extremely wet and uncomfortable, but fortunately there were some refreshments, which helped to alleviate the drooping spirits of the 'dripping anglers'.[3]

Some pubs like the Globe in Cranham Street, Jericho, reinforced local loyalties by setting up their own social clubs. Members of the Globe's club went to Buckland for their annual jaunt in July 1896, playing Aunt Sally and quoits before lunch and cricket in the afternoon.[4] Much more furtively in the face of police harassment, a few public houses maintained a link with prostitution and, in 1886, the appropriately named Bird in Hand beer-house in Cross Street lost its licence because it was 'a habitual resort of prostitutes'; one witness had trembled at her door to see 'soldiers and women leave the house with jars of beer on Sunday afternoons and go to Dover's-Row'.[5]

Outside the pub there were many other secular entertainments consisting largely of informal activities in and around the street and irregular commercial amusements such as circuses and fairs. In all but the busiest thoroughfares the street was still a place of recreation and, for many children, the only playground. In 1896, A Sufferer from Walton Crescent complained that youngsters gathered at the end of the street as soon as school was over,

indulging in such games as football, cricket, and hop-scotch (for which purpose they make chalk marks all over the pavement) to the annoyance of the people who reside in the neighbourhood. They also amuse themselves by climbing the railings of the front garden, and opening and shutting the gates. As many are lodging-houses for members of the University the noise is a great inconvenience to those gentlemen studying, and complaints out of number have been made to the police, but without any good result. People are continually swilling the pavements in front of their houses with water in the hope of keeping the children away, but as soon as they begin to get dry they return again. Only last week one of the householders, through a quarrel, had a large window broken with a flint stone.[6]

In 1880, a Cowley lad was fined for playing cricket in Stanley Road 'to the annoyance of the public'. He, together with six or eight others, had been playing there on Sundays for many weeks and PC Walker testified that 'The language they used was disgraceful and disgusting, and they could not speak without using oaths. . . . A tin was used for stumps.'[7] Away from the streets, men and boys clung to the habit of nude bathing in local rivers, a practice condemned in 1869 as 'annoying to ladies, who cannot indulge in a row on the water or even take a walk by the side of the river without encountering such disgraceful indecency.' Twenty years later, there were complaints that, on the Cherwell near St Clement's 'you may see naked young men roosting on a bridge or on the bank . . . and your ears are shocked with the most disgusting language.'[8] Gambling, another favourite pastime was driven into remoter areas by police vigilance. In 1868, up to 150 children were found playing pitch and toss on Sundays on the Thames footpath beyond St Ebbe's and, in 1895, nineteen lads were prosecuted for playing 'banker' on Port Meadow.[9] Wintry weather provided other recreational opportunities and, in December 1860 for example, an ice cricket match was played between the North Oxford and Britannia Clubs.[10] In January 1879, crowds flocked on to the ice at Christ Church Meadow, skating happily despite the thaw until

the ice suddenly gave way in all directions, and numerous immersions followed. Fortunately the water was not deep, but

notwithstanding this considerable difficulty was experienced in extricating several ladies, and one in particular could not be removed from her unpleasant position for some time, and serious consequences it was feared would result from cold and fright. The mishap was witnessed by a goodly company of spectators on the bank, and the ducking received by many individuals created considerable amusement.[11]

More wholesome entertainment, perhaps, was provided in the cold winters of 1853, 1891 and 1895 when the Thames froze so completely that a coach could be driven on the ice. In January 1891, James Porter, a livery stable keeper in St Aldate's, took a coach and four on to the river:

To prevent the horses slipping each shoe was fitted with six specially made nails, with heads shaped like a wedge, and these answered the purpose admirably. Mr James Porter handled the ribbons, and the passengers comprised his family. It is estimated that the total weight of the whole turn out was between six and seven tons. . . . Starting from opposite the University Barge, the coach was driven at a trot as far as the Long Bridges. Beyond that point it was not considered safe to proceed owing to the ice being of somewhat less strength, and the coach was therefore turned and driven back. The unusual spectacle, it is needless to say, attracted considerable attention from the skaters and others on the river, and . . . it is estimated there were between six and seven thousand persons congregated on the ice-bound river between Folly Bridge and the Cherwell, the greatest crush being near the University Barge.[12]

For spectators and participants alike, commercial amusements added their own highlights in the year. Until 1880, the Oxford Races on Port Meadow – held during the University's Long Vacation in August – brought to the city crowds of racegoers and accompanying card sharps, tricksters and extravagantly dressed bookmakers. Among the attractions in 1865 was:

Children gather round a Punch and Judy show at the corner of Castle Street and New Road in 1888. Informal street entertainments of this kind provided welcome amusement for the less well-off.

Coach and four on the Thames near Folly Bridge in 1891. This was a special event, but frozen rivers and meadows around the city provided fun for all – so much so that in December 1842, Mark Pattison complained that he had tried skating on the Isis but found it 'most unpoetically thronged with cads'.

THE WONDER OF THE AGE ! ! !

THE OXFORDSHIRE CALF,
As Exhibited at the Royal Cremorne Gardens
(fully Developed),
With Two Heads, Two Necks, Four Eyes,
Four Ears, Two Briskets, Two Back Bones,
Two Tails, Four Fore Legs, Two Hind Legs &c., &c.,
Admission 6d. each; Schools and Children half-price.[13]

Like the Oxford Races, St Giles' Fair had begun in the seventeenth century, but it developed during the Victorian period from a small pleasure fair into a major annual holiday for working people, including many who came from a distance by excursion trains. Florence Gamlen recalled the fair in the 1860s:

There would be a small circus and a dramatic company which produced a Triple Bill of tragedy, comedy and pantomime. Always a fat woman, a living skeleton, a giant, and dwarfs small enough to creep into a tiny two storied house and ring a bell out of its upper window; often Mermaids, who were apt to be stuffed seals and disappointing, and wax-works representing the more notable crowned Heads of Europe and the latest notorious criminals. One outstanding horror I still remember, a coal black negro, who ate live rats at intervals throughout one day, till the police interfered, when raw beefsteak was swallowed as a substitute. Cheap Jacks standing in front of their vans above the crowd offered amazing bargains, likely to involve them in great financial loss. Amazing patter and the ground bait of the sight of purses apparently containing more money than the price at which they were offered, collected a crowd of eager buyers, for whom disappointment generally lay in store. There were shooting galleries, coco-nut shies; comparatively safe, silent swings and roundabouts; the latter pushed by hand, provided little wooden horses for the adventurous, and little coaches for the young and timid.[14]

By the end of the 1880s, St Giles' Fair was both larger and noisier, offering steam-powered rides as well as the more traditional amusements:

The stalls extended on the west side from Little Clarendon Street to New-Inn-Hall Street. At the top of St Giles' Blandy's Ghost Illusions formed the attraction. In close proximity was a flying trapeze, which was a novelty. A thick wire was erected about 30 feet high and 40 yards long. To this was attached a handle with wheels, which with slight pressure ran swiftly down the wire. The public were invited to take hold of this handle, throw themselves from the platform, and then experience the peculiar sensation of flying through the air. At the end of the wire was a padded board to prevent injury to the aerialists, and a net underneath in case of a fall. This was well patronized, not by men and boys only, but on Monday by numerous females, who ascended the platform and made the flight quite regardless of the audible comments of the onlookers at their temerity. After a time the proprietor of the trapeze was informed that the journey would not be allowed to be undertaken by females. Day's menagerie, containing a collection of 500 animals, including lions, tigers, leopards, bears, hyaenas, pack of wild wolves, ostriches, pelicans, vultures, owls, &c., was filled from morning to night. Amongst the other shows were . . . two sparring saloons, the armless wonder (a man born without hands or arms), who performed all kinds of work with his feet, 'The Beauty of Adelaide', a woman of immense size, 'Kasper and Tamara', the mysterious thought readers, Carver's champion shooters (a man firing at apples, plums, &c., on a woman's head), Scott's circus, Anderton's conjuring entertainment, Sidgwick's menagerie and waxworks (including Lorenzo, an American lion tamer), the performing fleas, &c. The roundabouts were numerous, and included the old-fashioned ones turned with a handle to the latest improvements in steam-powered engines. . . . Two steam switchback railways should be included among the novelties. They were largely patronized by old and young, and the proprietors of 'the plant' will carry with them pleasant recollections of the fair. . . .

The Oxford Bible stall was, as usual, erected near St John's and Mr Wheelhouse and Commander Williams courteously received all comers. Tracts were freely distributed, and the Church Army held meetings in St Giles' on both days. . . . The majority of young people, as on previous occasions, amused themselves by brushing each other's faces with feather brushes. In a few cases where these were being roughly used the police deprived the owners of them. The attendance was extremely large on both days.[15]

St Giles' Fair and the small pleasure fairs held in Gloucester Green in May and St Clement's in September were fixtures in the local calendar; other commercial entertainments were less predictable, but equally popular. In Thomas Hughes' novel TOM BROWN AT OXFORD, the hero and other undergraduates disrupted a temporary menagerie that had been set up in Gloucester Green:

Inside they found an exciting scene. The place was pretty well lighted, and the birds and beasts were all alive in their several dens and cages, walking up and down, and each uttering remonstrances after its own manner, the shrill notes of birds mingling with the moan of the beasts of prey and chattering of the monkeys. Feeding time had been put off till night to suit the undergraduates, and the undergraduates were proving their appreciation of the attention by playing off all manner of practical jokes on birds and beasts, their keepers, and such of the public as had been rash enough to venture in. At the farther end was the keeper, who did the showman, vainly endeavouring to go through his usual jogtrot description. His monotone was drowned every minute by the chorus of voices, each shouting out some new fact in natural history touching the biped or quadruped whom the keeper was attempting to describe. . . . A small and indignant knot of townspeople, headed by a stout and severe middle-aged woman, with two big boys her sons, followed the keeper, endeavouring by caus-

tic remarks and withering glances to stop the flood of chaff, and restore the legitimate authority and the reign of keeper and natural history.[16]

In August 1861, the tight-rope walker Blondin attracted up to five thousand people to a field in Holywell where he performed various daring exploits on a rope fixed between two tall uprights.[17] Circuses regularly visited Oxford and set up their marquees in convenient suburban fields. In June 1861, for instance, Newsome's Alhambra Circus opened in Cowley Road, offering seats at prices ranging from 1 guinea for a private box to 6d. for a place in the gallery. JACKSON'S OXFORD JOURNAL was highly impressed by 'the variety and quality of the entertainments, and the very admirable and orderly manner in which they are conducted.' Success was assured,

not only with the humbler, but with the richer class of our fellow citizens and families, for there is nothing . . . which could possibly give offence even to the most fastidious.[18]

By the end of Victoria's reign, much larger circuses were coming to town and, in 1898, Barnum and Bailey's Circus included a great menagerie and a 'freak' show. The circus performances took place in a huge tent seating up to twelve thousand people with three large rings and two expansive stages with a wide quarter-mile track running round them:

Everything that appertains to the circus was there, and much more. There was the best of everything and everything of the best. Interest was never allowed to diminish for one moment. All sorts of tumblers and somersaulters appeared, clowns kept up a roar of laughter, and surprising jockey acts were rendered by numerous members of both sexes. At one time the air was full of trapezists, at another horses held the ring and demonstrated their remarkable training. Not only horses, but animals of lower estate, down to the humble pig, were called upon to contribute to the fun and enjoyment. The supreme equestrian act was that for which Mr William Dacrow was responsible.

St Giles' Fair in 1868 when it still consisted largely of freak shows, swings, hand-powered roundabouts, cheap-jacks and stalls selling fairings.

Headington Quarry Cricket Club in about 1910. Churches and chapels provided many recreational opportunities and sporting clubs were often started by energetic churchmen as a way of promoting 'Muscular Christianity'.

Horse after horse was brought into the ring, over which he held command, until at last they numbered seventy. Seated on a lovely white horse on a pedestal, which occupied the centre of the ring, he put the others through a series of remarkable evolutions. . . .

After the circus came the hippodrome races round the track at break-neck speed; but, for pure danger and excitement, the Roman double team standing race was conspicuous. The chariot races first with pairs and then with four horses, continued the excitement. Away the horses sped, the chariots clattering behind them, and the drivers holding on like grim death. Every possible bit of speed was got out of the animals, which seemed to enter into the spirit of the races, and flew along round the curve and up the straight until the apportioned distance was covered, and the prize awarded. Jumping exhibitions, coursing contests with Whippet racing dogs, double three horse tandem hurdle races, and a sprinting contest also appeared on the programme.[19]

To these traditional amusements, churches and middle-class reformers sought to add 'rational recreation', regulated entertainment which would help to divert working men from the pub and expose them to a superior example. Their motives included a basic humanitarianism and fear of political unrest, but for local churches and chapels, the provision of recreation facilities became a 'civilizing mission to the poor'. In Cowley St John, for example, Revd W.J. Priest, curate in the late 1860s, introduced many innocent recreations such as the winter lectures and entertainments which were held weekly in the Princes Street Schoolroom from 1867. In 1868 he founded a horticultural society and went on to establish a musical society, a parish lending library and reading-rooms which were set up in parish schoolrooms.[20] In Holy Trinity parish, the vicar and curate opened coffee rooms in 1877:

Coffee, tea, and cocoa are provided at one half-penny, or one penny per cup, and cake or bread and butter at the same rate. All are welcome to a comfortable, warm, and cheerful room, free of cost and . . . the rooms are full every evening from 5 till 10 pm, when all depart, and instead of rolling, walk to their homes as steady as a soldier on march. By this means have men been drawn from the ale house and its evil consequences, others from the streets, where swearing, quarrelling, and fighting was the order of proceeding, for the want of something better to do or a room to sit in.[21]

Other churchmen organized penny readings, spelling bees and even a musical bee, although in this latter case, the vicar of St Frideswide's, Revd G.L. Kemp, insisted on hearing the words of every song before the event.[22]

Churches and chapels also tried to influence their parishioners through the development of organized sport on the public school and university model. An early proponent of this 'Muscular Christianity' in Oxford was the vicar of St Barnabas', Revd M.H. Noel, who felt that 'the church should be the centre of everything – of worship, of education and of amusement as well.'[23] His parish soon had cricket, association football and rugby football teams and the cricket club successfully challenged SS Philip and James CC in July 1873:

St Phillip's went first to the wickets and totalled 87, Messrs. Adam and Phillips each playing a good innings. The St Barnabas' fielding, with one or two exceptions, was very weak. Their innings, too, commenced badly, the chief object of the batsmen apparently being to run each other out. Five wickets had fallen for 16 runs, when a stand was made by Tipton and the St Barnabas' Captain, whose obstinate defence for above an hour brought on repeated changes of bowling, and slowly raised the score to 80. Five runs were yet required when the last man went in, and amidst great excitement they were made by Cross and A. Money.[24]

The facilities provided by churchmen were multiplied by philanthropists, employers and other agencies. In St Clement's for instance, the young Balliol philosopher, T.H. Green, and Revd Arthur Butler, Dean of Oriel College, helped to set up a British Workman Club in 1875.[25]

For employers, the provision of recreational opportunities combined apparent generosity with the search for industrial efficiency; in Oxford, this so-called 'Welfare Capitalism' was most evident at the University Press where Thomas Combe established a band in the 1850s to supply employees

with the means of amusing themselves in an intelligent and manly way, and of uniting them together by means of musical fraternity, and of binding them to their employers by some signs of personal attachment and interest in their welfare.[26]

Many firms organized annual treats for their workforces and, in August 1870, the city police had a particularly unfortunate outing to Nuneham Park:

The party, in two barges, left Oxford at about half-past ten o'clock in the morning, and, on arriving at Nuneham, wickets were pitched for a match between the City and County Forces. Football was also set going, and trap-bat-and-ball engaged in; whilst a quadrille band, under the direction of Mr Freebarn, and the Kidlington Brass Band, supplied music to the dancers, many preferring this mode of enjoying themselves. Before cricket had been played long, ominous showers set in, and the party adjourned to dinner in the hopes of better weather. Dinner over, it was determined to proceed with the game in spite of the rain, but, after a little experience of its effects, the match was declared drawn, although the advantage lay with the City Force. Seeing no prospect of fine weather, the return voyage was begun, and, as the saloons of both barges were crowded by half-drenched people, it must have been a relief when the party arrived at Folly Bridge.[27]

While other recreation facilities proliferated, local authorities which prided themselves on the city's low rates came under increasing pressure to provide or improve social amenities. Thus, in the early 1850s, the corporation was persuaded to establish a public library to encourage the moral and intellectual improvement of the working classes who had

'nothing but the attractions of the ale-house or the blandishments of pleasure'.[28] *Opened in June 1854, the library remained a very low priority and, even after it was re-housed in the new Town Hall in the 1890s, its stock attracted severe criticism:*

We have fine rooms, but a miserably scanty supply of books. Contrast the 9,458 volumes – including magazines – in our Library, with the magnificent collection of Cambridge, 43,909, and Cheltenham, 27,980; and of these books of ours, what a mass of old rubbish takes up shelf room and repels readers! A glance at the A.B.C. card indicator in the Reference Library will show that in many departments, if not indeed in all, Oxford cannot be said to have a Reference Library at all. Of modern technical works on sciences and arts there is a most discreditable lack. For Physics, for instance, no text book later than 1832, for Arithmetic 1857, for Architecture 1849, for Engineering the same date, for Agriculture there is a text book on 'the new system adopted in 1726', Mechanics, Natural History (represented by Goldsmith's *History of the Earth!*), Medicine, Anatomy, all tell the same tale, all bring contributions to a pile of ancient rubbish. The science of Chemistry closes in 1822, Geology in 1859, and taking even the humble but useful guide books, France is treated from the standpoint of 1854, and 'Modern London' is described in 1857. . . . Surely it would even be better to show empty shelves, and invite the charitable to clothe their nakedness, than hoard and index a useless collection of rubbish.[29]

In 1846, frequent drownings and the immodesty of nude bathers on the river banks compelled the corporation to provide a river bathing place in St Ebbe's. A second bathing place was provided to the north of Osney at Tumbling Bay in 1853, but it was not until the mid-1880s that pressure from East Ward ratepayers forced the Local Board to arrange temporary use of the University bathing place at Long Bridges during Long Vacations.[30] The bathing places were exclusively for males until 1891 when women were allowed to use Tumbling Bay

Members of the Oxford University Press players in January 1894. The Press was a keen provider of recreational facilities for its employees and, in 1893, it built the Clarendon Press Institute in Walton Street at a cost of £5,000.

The Jolly Farmer's public house in Paradise Street in 1906. Shuffrey's painting depicts a Town pub which served the community living near the County Gaol and within a few yards of Victorian Oxford's largest breweries, Hall's and Morrell's.

St Thomas's church from the south-east, a study by C.H. Spiers in 1871. Situated in a poor and populous neighbourhood and increasingly hemmed in by railway sidings and commercial development, St Thomas's churchyard retained a surprisingly rural character.

on Fridays;[31] in August 1900, after a petition from over 1,700 women, a bathing place for women was opened at Long Bridges although the men downstream complained about 'bathing in water in which the fair sex have already disported themselves'.[32]

Municipal inertia was also seen in the case of parks and recreation grounds. The formation of the University Parks in the 1860s and the continued availability of Christ Church Meadow helped to justify this inaction, but access to these places was restricted to 'respectable' citizens who refrained from objectionable activities. In 1867, Charles Dodgson regretted the exclusion of ordinary folk in his poem THE DESERTED PARKS:

How often have I loitered o'er thy green,
Where humble happiness endeared the scene!
How often have I paused on every charm,
The rustic couple walking arm in arm –
The groups of trees, with seats beneath the shade
For prattling babes and whisp'ring lovers made –
The never-failing brawl, the busy mill
Where tiny urchins vied in fistic skill –
(Two phrases only have that dusky race
Caught from the learned influence of the place;
Phrases in their simplicity sublime,
'Scramble a copper!' 'Please, Sir, what's the time?')
These round thy walks their cheerful influence shed;
There were thy charms – but all these charms are fled.
Amidst thy bowers the tyrant's hand is seen,
And rude pavilions sadden all thy green;
One selfish pastime grasps the whole domain,
And half a faction swallows up the plain;
Adown thy glades, all sacrificed to cricket,
The hollow-sounding bat now guards the wicket;
Sunk are thy mounds in shapeless level all,
Lest aught impede the swiftly rolling ball;
And trembling, shrinking from the fatal blow,
Far, far away thy hapless children go.

Ill fares the place, to luxury a prey,
Where wealth accumulates, and minds decay;
Athletic sports may flourish or may face,
Fashion may make them even as it has made;
But the broad parks, the city's joy and pride,
When once destroyed can never be supplied![33]

In an amusing incident in May 1896, the exclusive character of the Parks seriously annoyed the Oxford MP, Viscount Valentia, when the head constable refused his request to admit the Yeomanry Band:

Lord Valentia argued the point with the head constable, who, however, was firm in refusing to depart from his orders. He pointed out to the noble lord, amid the laughter of the crowd which had assembled, that if he so far departed from his instructions as to admit the Yeomanry Band without an order, he might be asked the next day to admit a German band. A suggestion was made by one of the officers that the band should force their way through, but the Park officials at once closed the gates. Eventually a messenger was dispatched to the Rev H.J. Bidder, one of the curators, who gave a written permission for the Band to enter, which permission of course produced the desired effect.[34]

In August 1892 the City Council was at last shamed into spending up to £50 on establishing a temporary and experimental recreation ground for East Ward on a remote field beside the Cowley Road. Its success was hardly unqualified, since vandalism forced the removal of the swings and other equipment on Sundays and, at night, the place was the resort of 'horrible prostitutes'.[35] Henry Taunt lived opposite and, in August 1897, he wrote to the Council complaining about the stile at the entrance:

This is a thorough nuisance – the high stile prevents old people, ladies and young children from getting into the recreation ground, the broad top rail is utilized by young roughs in the

Paddling in the river opposite the college barges in the 1890s. Oxford's waterways were a free playground in summer, although respectable folk were offended by the prevalence of nude bathing.

day time as a vantage point on which to sit and slang their mates and the passers-by and at night it is used for purposes which are usually done in dark corners. . . .[36]

The Council made no further experiments with recreation grounds during Victoria's reign, but during the mayoralty of T.H. Kingerlee in 1899, a series of open air concerts was staged in various parts of Oxford, beginning in St Ebbe's:

Here, about half-past seven on Tuesday evening the waiting crowds were favoured with a view of a heavy van which was driven rapidly up and brought to a standstill underneath a gas lamp, followed by a handcart on which reposed a pianoforte. A British workman with a broom was next con-jured up, and, having ejected a stray dog who had taken up his position on the van, proceeded to gently sweep the sur-face. From somewhere else appeared a carpet, and long before the hour to begin had arrived a strong and ornamen-tal impromptu platform had been arranged. Meanwhile the crowd began to grow denser and denser until, when the programme was opened, there were about a thousand per-sons present, the younger element being present in force. The pit was the flinty road, the promenade balcony was the path, the gallery which was occupied by the irrepressible 'encore boys', was the high wall, and probably no gathering was ever more enjoyable. . . .[37]

If the City Council was reluctant to spend money on purely recre-ational matters, it proved much more responsive to the demand for allotments in the late 1880s. The issue aroused strong feelings among 'the industrious and respectable poor' and there was extensive middle-class support for a movement which could only encourage thrift and self-improvement. The vicars of St Frideswide's and New Hinksey, for example, were prominent supporters of allotments and the Revd W.B. Duggan, vicar of St Paul's felt that it was good for Oxford to encourage 'the sober, refining, meditative work of the garden and of the seed plots'.[38] Sites were soon provided and in August

1891 the Osney Allotments Association held its first annual show in an adjoining field, complete with swingboats, coconuts, Aunt Sally and music from the City Police Band.[39]

With the introduction of bank holidays in 1871 and a general reduction in working hours, many people had increasing leisure time and might prefer to organize it themselves. The railways offered all but the poorest access to recreation, beauty and quiet. During the summer of 1855, there were excursions from Oxford to Bath and Bristol, to Brighton, to Wychwood Forest Fair and to Epsom Races; the OXFORD CHRONICLE *pointed out that these trains were 'the only means of recreation and enjoyment available to the working and middle classes of the community. . . .'[40]*

Within Oxford, horse trams offered easier access to the surrounding countryside, but, in the 1890s, the bicycle gave much greater freedom to all who could afford to buy one. In the suburbs, greater space in and around the home encouraged the development of personal hobbies such as gardening, woodwork and the breeding and keeping of animals, fish or birds. Reading was everywhere encouraged by improved education and the spread of cheap literature and locally also by the opening of a lending department within Oxford City Library in 1857.[41] A pas-sion for music was fostered by the availability of cheaper instruments although this could have unfortunate consequences for neighbours. In 1893, 'A Respectable Ratepayer' in Grandpont was threatening to dynamite the piano next door because it was played from 6 a.m. to 10 p.m. by the eleven girls in the family.[42]

Recreational providers clearly hoped that the profusion of opportu-nities would gradually 'civilize' the whole community but it is evident that many people resisted this influence. Disruptive elements were often present at improving lectures and, in December 1869, for exam-ple, there was trouble at a Cowley St John entertainment when the lecture on astrology proved over-long:

A set of rude unmannerly boys, and many young men, who ought to have set a better example, created considerable dis-turbance, greeting the lecturer's homely illustrations with shouts of laughter and rattling chairs on the floor in their impatience for the second part of the entertainment.[43]

Elementary schoolchildren celebrate the Queen's Diamond Jubilee in the University Parks in 1897. They were given special jubilee medals and, during the course of the afternoon, they managed to consume 1,400 gallons of tea, 21 cwt of cake and 14 cwt of biscuits.

In 1890, unruly boys were making it 'impossible to stay and read quietly' in the City Library and 'what with the tobacco smoke and the pushing about and the pulling of hair' the promenade concerts in the Corn Exchange were felt to be unsuitable for respectable girls in 1899.[44] In January 1888, during a Cowley St John Working Men's Club football match, the curate of the parish, the Revd Carpenter, was annoyed by trespassing youths who were playing nearby and 'using most disgraceful language':

Mr Carpenter reproved them in a playful manner, boxing one boy's ear, when two brothers set upon him in a very insulting manner, fighting, kicking, and using such oaths as bargemen would shun, being backed up by other youths, ages from 16 years downwards. Mr Carpenter very humanely kept them at bay, refusing proffered aid, thinking, no doubt, the police were the proper authorities to interfere, knowing, and afterwards finding out the kind of people the parents of the boys were.[45]

An incident in Jericho in April 1899 where a policeman came upon two drunken men fighting in the midst of a large crowd[46] showed that, in the poorer areas at least, little had really changed.

CHAPTER TWELVE

Town and Gown

The Bargee came up furious, and hit out wildly at Charles Larkyns; but science was more than a match for brute force; and, after receiving two or three blows which caused him to shake his head in a don't-like-it sort of way, he endeavoured to turn his attention to Mr Verdant Green, who, with head in air, was taking the greatest care of his spectacles, and endeavouring to ward off the indiscriminate lunges of half a dozen townsmen. The Bargee's charitable designs on our hero were, however, frustrated by the opportune appearance of Mr Blades and Mr Cheke, the gentleman-commoner of Corpus, who, in their turn, were closely followed by Mr Smalls and Mr Flexible Shanks; and Mr Blades exclaiming, 'There's a smasher for your ivories, my fine fellow!' followed up the remark with a practical application of his fist to the part referred to; whereupon the Bargee fell back with a howl, and gave vent to several curse-ory observations, and blank remarks.[1]

Cuthbert Bede's fictional account of a Guy Fawkes' night battle between Town and Gown paints a traditional picture of relations between the two sides. Such incidents were by no means uncommon and, in the 1830s, George Denison of Oriel College was knocked to the ground by a stone during a pitched battle outside Balliol College:

Mr dear old friend, the then Master of Balliol, Dr Jenkyns, was just sitting down to dinner. He said, – 'What is all this disturbance outside?' – 'Master, it is a great fight – Town and Gown; and they say that Mr Denison of Oriel is killed.' He said – 'Give me my Academicals and open the door of the house into the street.' The household represented the danger of doing this. The answer was – 'Give me my Academicals, and open the door.' The master stood on the doorsteps and had just said to Town, – 'My deluded friends' when a heavy stone was pitched into the middle of his body and he fell back into the arms of his servants, crying out, 'Close the door'.[2]

A similar fate befell the mayor, Thomas Randall, during disturbances on 5 November 1859:

Symptoms of a quarrelsome nature began to manifest themselves shortly before 9 o'clock, when about 500 or 600 undergraduates mustered in a body in the streets, which they paraded in a most defiant manner, shouting 'Gown, Gown'. Shortly afterwards the cry of 'Town, Town', was heard, and an immense number of mechanics and others showed a bold front, and a regular row ensued which it is impossible to describe. . . . The Mayor was knocked down, the ex-Mayor and Alderman Sadler were pushed and jostled; and such was the determination evinced by the undergraduates for fighting that the special constables were compelled to use their staves, which they did to some effect upon the heads and shoulders of those University men who came in contact with them. In the High-street, at the house of Mr Embling, a gownsman, who was lodging there, opened his window for the purpose of

A Town and Gown disturbance on 5 November, which served as an annual excuse for renewed hostilities between the old enemies. On this occasion, the scene of battle was outside Balliol College near St Mary Magdalen church.

haranguing the towns people, but on his making use of insulting words a volley of stones smashed nearly the whole of his three windows.[3]

The bread riots of November 1867 gave University Volunteers official sanction to attack townsmen:

The University men, some hundreds strong, were permitted, at their own particular desire, to be in the van, and I shall never forget their swift and joyous onrush. In a spirit of the keenest enjoyment, with an ecstatic shout, they fell upon the mob in front of them with irresistible determination, and mowed them down as though they had been grass. In fancy, I can hear now the rapping of the staves upon the heads of the discomfited disturbers, intermingled with the cries of the wounded. I never heard anything more like a wholesale cracking of nuts than it was, and this simile is appropriate enough in view of the fact that it was human nuts which were in the grip of the crackers. The rioters, quite unprepared for such an onslaught, made but a feeble resistance, and in a very few minutes turned and ignominiously fled.[4]

Open warfare between Town and Gown tended to diminish during Victoria's reign, but townsfolk were often scandalized by student rowdyism. In April 1872, for example, H.B. protested that his visit to a panorama of the Franco–Prussian War had been ruined as soon as half-a-dozen undergraduates arrived:

They immediately commenced the most hideous yells from each side of the house, thrusting their ungainly feet over the front of the boxes, desisting everything, and insulting the proprietor with the coarsest remarks. One youth actually snatched the boot from his friend's foot and hurled it at the box opposite; another threw it up at the gas, and finally it fell among the audience in the pit.[5]

More general disorder occurred in May 1897 during the visit of the Prince of Wales. Crowds thronged the streets in the evening to see the illuminations, but

Locomotion was much impeded by the boisterous and unruly behaviour of undergraduates, who paraded the streets arm-in-arm or in gangs, and by dint of vigorous and frequent rushes swept all before them, making matters not only unpleasant, but really dangerous for all but the most active. . . . Women and children were knocked down in all directions, and the behaviour of many undergraduates was positively disgraceful.

So violent and outrageous was their conduct that it can only be accounted for by the assumption that they had imbibed too freely at dinner. The crush at Carfax when the mob passed backwards and forwards was so great as to be at times quite dangerous, and it required all the efforts of the mounted police to prevent serious injury being done to life and property.[6]

In the subsequent uproar, F.E. Smith, Fellow of Merton and the future Lord Birkenhead, was arrested after intervening to stop his scout's lad from being roughly handled by the police.[7]

If there was less actual fighting between Town and Gown, there lingered an atmosphere of mutual enmity. In 1871, for instance, the University periodical DARK BLUE was sneeringly dismissive of Oxford's civic representatives:

The local board of this – the most beautiful city of the empire – is composed mainly of the most ignorant of petty tradesmen, plus a small and unwilling minority of University representatives. It is hardly credible that men of intellectual calibre and exalted status – such as the Dean of Christ Church and Warden of New College – should be compelled to endure the ungrammatical insolence of small mob-orators elected under the pseudonym Liberal, in reality the most stolid of stopgaps. . . . Oxford exists for the University. It would therefore be no more than a sentimental hardship if the disposition of the city were in the hands of the University entirely. If we must be saddled with obstructives, let them at least be educated, and therefore amenable to reason.[8]

Owen Gamlen, the Chief Constable of Oxfordshire, had a chilly reception in University society because 'There was then scarcely any intercourse between the University and professional families.'[9] Still less contact existed between the University and Trade and, as a child, Naomi Mitchison was

severely lectured about trade when I was discovered to have made friends behind the counter at the small draper's in North Parade. There were little drawers with buttons and hooks and silk or cotton thread which I had been allowed to look into delightedly and touch, better than a doll's house. I was made to feel naughty, but worst was having to pretend not to be friends with the ladies in the black stuff dresses, to be made to feel they were somehow different, that they 'smelled'.[10]

In these circumstances, there was a good deal of ill-feeling between the haves and have-nots and, in North Parade, the children of the have-nots were always on the look-out for unattended 'University children':

Jumping about with excitement and pointing with their fingers they shouted 'gentry' with such scorn and contempt as almost to imply *à la lanterne!* 'Cads' called back a breathless victim sprinting for safety.[11]

Against this background of underlying hostility, Town and Gown were actually working more closely together in administering the growing city. The principle of joint action on statutory bodies had been adopted in 1771 when equal numbers of City and University representatives were appointed to the Oxford Paving Commission and the Oxford Market Committee. In 1877, Professor Montagu Burrows praised a wise policy which reminded him of a way of effecting reconciliation between quarrelling married couples:

They shut the man and wife up into a room for a fortnight, with one bed, one table, one chair, one plate, one spoon. (Laughter.) If at the end of that time they had not made it up, the divorce was granted. But the plan generally succeeded. This was what had been done with us. In the Local Board, the Guardianship of the Poor, the Police Committee, and smaller bodies – to say nothing of the School Board – delegates from both bodies sat side by side and worked harmoniously. Their interests were the same, their public spirit was the same, and long might that harmony continue.[12]

Policemen from the joint City and University force outside the police station at Kemp Hall in about 1895. The University paid two-fifths of the cost of the force when it was set up in 1869, but succeeded in reducing its share to one-third in 1881.

Not everyone shared this view and, in 1872, the Oxford solicitor, R.S. Hawkins, felt that

The time was coming when 2,000 members of the University must merge into the 30,000 citizens; and such a merging would be for the public advantage. At the discussions of these public bodies the personal interests of these corporations came in the way of the public good. The time was coming when if they had University members in the governing bodies those members must be elected as other representatives were, by the burgesses.[13]

From the University's point of view, increasing costs rather than democratic scruples proved the major incentive to try and disengage itself from some aspects of local government. In 1867, Town and Gown therefore found their historic roles reversed as the University tried to return the control of policing to an unwilling corporation:

The truth is that, with the growth of municipal liberties and the extension of the city, the cherished privilege of the University has become a mere burden, and a very costly one; while to the town the long-vexed question of the control of its police has ceased to be a matter of humiliation, and the concession of its opponents presents itself only in the unattractive guise of a threatened increase of its rates.[14]

A joint police force founded by both parties solved this particular problem in 1869, but a more general solution was only reached twenty years later. In November 1889, following the Local Government Act of 1888, most of Oxford's joint statutory bodies were replaced by an enlarged Oxford Corporation which had one-fifth of its representatives elected by the University and colleges.[15] By the end of the century, 'Cordial goodwill' was said to exist between City and University councillors[16] and in 1897, the Mayor of Oxford, Robert Buckell, was awarded an honorary MA degree.

Apart from its formal role in local government, the University was also involved in many aspects of Oxford life. Through ownership of much of the land in and around the city, the University and colleges were, for example, in a position to influence the very development of the place.

On the urban fringe St John's College could pursue a long-term strategy of developing a high-class suburb in North Oxford; in East Oxford, by contrast, the major concern of Christ Church was 'to prevent the building of shabby or unsightly houses within view of the Meadow and path.'[17] In 1852, the college received a report from Henry Bailey, Lord Harcourt's gardener at Nuneham, about 'defensive' tree-planting in Iffley Road:

There is a very pretty point of view . . . where Merton Tower and the Radcliffe is seen and where you propose leaving an opening; but I do not know how this is to be managed with a view to concealing from Ch Ch (sic) Meadow the cottages which you anticipate by the side of the road, unless you could secure the sites of three or four of them and plant a few trees on the opposite side of the opening.'[18]

In central Oxford, college and University landownership facilitated the clearance of old properties for commercial development and for large building projects such as the building of the Examination Schools (1876–82). In St Thomas's, Christ Church, as major landowner, was able to embark on ambitious re-housing schemes, erecting model dwellings on the site of 'some of the worst tenements which could be found in Oxford.'[19]

With the increasing use of lodging-houses, especially to accommodate poorer students, the University became concerned with housing standards in many private homes and established the Delegacy of Lodging-Houses in 1868. There were several anxieties about the lodging-houses system and, in 1876 for instance, Dean Burgon expressed fears that close proximity between undergraduates and young female servants 'must needs be in a high degree demoralizing (and) cannot fail to lead to mischievous consequences.'[20] Five years earlier DARK BLUE had attacked the rapacity of the Oxford landlady:

'Honestly if you care to, but – get money.' Such is the motto of the average Oxford lodging keeper. . . . Rent, considering accommodation offered and required, is exorbitant, peculation systematic. A female there is doing a thriving business, who accumulates her little profit in the following honourable and wholesome manner. Undergraduates occupy all her rooms. *De rigueur* most of them own dogs. These clean-mouthed quadrupeds she contracts to feed at from three to four shillings per tail per week. The staple of diet is of course bones, which the dogs scrape with that assiduity for which the canine race is remarkable. Then the good soul collects them, and they make excellent soup for the unwary lodger at sixpence per basin. Verily this is sharing your bone with your dog in most utilitarian fashion![21]

The sanitary state of the lodging-houses most concerned the University authorities and it became a national issue in December 1880 after an undergraduate in lodgings died of diphtheria. His grieving father wrote to THE TIMES, *warning all young men of 'the poisonous condition that awaited them in Oxford' and recalling that his son had complained of 'the stink of the lodgings'.[22] The Delegacy quickly appointed a sanitary officer to advise and report upon all licensed lodging-houses and, in the spring of 1881, a chartered engineer, E.F.G. Griffith, inspected all 612 properties, finding only twenty-one that needed no improvement. Griffith stirred up a veritable hornet's nest of opposition and, in February 1882, complained that*

every obstacle has been put in my way, not so much by the tenants as by the landlords, and everything that has been done has been carried out under protest, even the workmen themselves sharing in this general feeling of prejudice against the alterations.[23]

Nevertheless, lodging-house keepers had no choice but to accept the Delegacy's terms if they were to retain their licences and most of them reluctantly did so.

Less formally, the University was also active in the fields of poor relief, education and health care. Most Oxford charities relied heavily upon University support and University men dominated the Charity

Robert Buckell in his mayoral robes in 1897. Originally a coal merchant, he later became an estate agent and the leading Liberal on the City Council. While he was mayor in 1897, he was awarded an honorary Master of Arts degree by the University in a gesture of conciliation.

Organization Society which was founded under the chairmanship of Col. W.E. Sackville West, Bursar of Keble, in 1873. Well-known Oxford figures such as William Spooner and L.R. Phelps, the Provost of Oriel, were prominent in a society which set out to reduce outdoor relief, offering help to the 'deserving' poor and leaving the rest to face the workhouse. Following the University Rating Act of 1854, the University and colleges were forced to contribute to the local poor rates and University representatives joined the Oxford Board of Guardians.[24] In education, the University ceased to maintain the Greycoat School in Jericho at the end of 1865 because the growth of parish schools had reduced attendances.[25] Individual colleges, however, continued to support local schools on their estates by donating sites – as Brasenose College did in Grandpont in 1891[26] – or subscribing towards building funds; in October 1872, for example, St John's gave £50 for the building of SS Philip and James' School.[27] Individual members of the University gained election to Oxford School Board from 1871 and the Balliol philosopher, T.H. Green was prominent in the foundation of the City of Oxford High School for Boys in 1881.[28] Green also supported the Wesleyan School in New Inn Hall Street, and, in St Clement's, helped to found the British Workman as a temperance alternative to the pub where he encouraged his friends to run a night school. In December 1875, he reported that

great credit was due to them. He was told that from 20 to 30 young men came very regularly and learnt a great deal, but it was found difficult to make much of some of them because they were so riotous and ignorant to begin with.[29]

Robert Horton, Fellow of New College, taught regularly at the Oxford Ragged School in St Ebbe's and tried to involve his friend John Marriott on one or two occasions. Marriott later recalled:

I could not cope with the boys, who were the rudest and roughest lot I ever encountered even in the 'worst' districts in either of my constituencies. Horton considerably condoned my miserable incapacity and released me from an ungrateful task. Even he himself confessed that the boys of St Ebbe's were 'simple savages'.

One Sunday they stoned him, but, as he characteristically added in recounting his experience: 'it is a blessed thought that a cup of cold water given to them is given to Christ.'[30]

The development of health care in Victorian Oxford owed much to people connected with the University. Until 1848, the Radcliffe Infirmary was entirely managed by the University and many subsequent improvements – for example, a fever ward in 1866 and a children's ward the following year – relied on the support and encouragement of men such as Dr Henry Acland and Professor George Rolleston.[31] Mrs Combe, widow of Thomas Combe, the superintendent of the University Press, provided funding for a new fever block and a children's ward at the Infirmary in 1877.[32] In the 1860s, she helped Eleanor Smith, the sister of Professor Henry Smith, to establish the first district nursing service in Oxford.[33] After the death of Henry Acland's wife Sarah, in 1878, district nursing was put on a permanent footing in the city when a group of her friends helped to raise money for the Acland Nursing Home.[34] The indefatigable Henry Acland was a leading figure in the establishment of the Cutler Boulter Provident Dispensary which opened in 1887, offering medical attention in return for a subscription of a few pennies a week.[35]

Some leading University figures had an important influence on the political life of Victorian Oxford. T.H. Green took a real interest in local politics and was the first don to sit on the city council, being elected for the North Ward as a Liberal in 1876.[36] Professor Montagu Burrows was a tireless worker for the Conservative cause and later recalled an amusing electoral experience:

On the first trial of strength, our weakness lay not only in our scanty list of supporters, but in the absurd timidity of some, especially in North Oxford, where our Villa-Conservatives were afraid of being mobbed, never having before recorded their votes. Their alarm was in some degree justified by the action of the enemy, who sent a wagon up to St Giles' School room, where the votes of the North were to be given, full of jeering youths in Radical colours, who shouted as every supposed Conservative came up. Observing this proceeding, I

The site of the Angel Hotel in High Street, cleared in 1876 to make way for the building of the Examination Schools. Ownership of much of this site by just three colleges made it easier for the University to proceed with this major scheme.

Excavations on the site of the city wall in 1899. Interested University dons stimulated the growth of historical societies and encouraged archaeological investigations like this dig beside the Bodleian Library.

ran down to Gloucester-Green, where I knew that election mobs assembled. I was looking about for some 'blues' when a fine hearty-looking man came up to me and asked what Captain Burrows wanted. 'Could he help me?' 'Yes,' said I, 'I want a dozen Tory roughs to come up to St Giles' polling place, and to shout down the red roughs in the wagon, who had had as yet their own way.' 'To be sure,' said he; 'wait five minutes and you shall have them.' In less time than that there they were, capital young fellows, up to anything. 'Form a line,' said my friend, 'right face; march.' I guided them; they drew up at the gate. The Radical wagon thought it best to drive off, and my poor frightened sheep took courage.[37]

In 1880, Burrows' determination to win the seat for the Conservative Alexander Hall led to desperate measures and a letter to the public orator, T.F. Dallin:

Dear Dallin

I found a note from Dayman when I got home last night saying the fight must collapse unless we can provide £500 over the Carlton £3,000. By same post I got a letter from Hathaway, saying he will come up and fight the election for us, and urging us to go on (from private information he has received of our good chances). Noel also promises to work Jericho this time. I look on these two helpers as worth 100 additional votes. We are sure to win. The thing must be settled before 11 am. So I see nothing for it but to come forward and guarantee £50 myself on condition H. Morrell, Parsons, and West bring £300 more by 11 to-day; but I must have help, and should like to raise my guarantee to £100. Can you aid me with £10 towards this sum? It is a crisis, and we must really sacrifice something for our party. Let me know by 10 am at All Souls, or by 11 am at Dayman and Walsh's office.

Yours sincerely
M Burrows[38]

Hall won the bye election, but Burrows' letter was found in the High Street by a little boy and led to the appointment of an election commission. Bribery on a large scale was revealed, Hall was unseated and Oxford was left without an MP until 1885.

The University also affected the recreational life of Oxford. Major sporting and social events not only attracted spectators but also encouraged imitation in the form of city athletic sports and regattas. During vacations, college sporting facilities and equipment were made available to college servants' teams and respectable city organizations. In term-time, undergraduates regularly provided popular entertainments for townsfolk such as those organized by the University Temperance Society at the Town Hall in February 1880.[39] In 1888, the Oxford Boys' Brigade was established by a member of the University 'to keep the boys off the streets'; the President, Col. Impey hoped to

enlist the sympathies of the citizens of Oxford. It is evident that however valuable is the aid of University men, such aid is only transient, and volunteer officers are wanted from the good men and true of this City, so that at least one officer of each company should be an Oxford townsman and a permanent resident, and I trust this appeal may not be in vain.[40]

If Oxonians generally benefited from these various facilities, they were deprived of regular theatrical performances by the University veto on professional drama in term-time until Jowett lifted the ban in 1883. For many years, the old Victoria Theatre had provided 'a glorified barn . . . for low-class representations of every kind', and good theatrical companies had to visit Oxford in vacations and cope with makeshift accommodation in the Town Hall, the Corn Exchange or other temporary venues.[41] At last, in February 1886, the New Theatre opened with an Oxford University Dramatic Society production of TWELFTH NIGHT. A new era of entertainment had dawned in Oxford, but one member of the audience was less than happy after leaning against some wet paint:

The cast of the OUDS production of The Taming of the Shrew *outside the New Theatre in 1897. Both Town and Gown benefited from the relaxation of the ban on term-time drama, leading as it did to the establishment of regular theatre in Oxford.*

Being asked by an inquisitive person whether 'he could stick the show once more', he replied with some asperity that he was already 'stuck'. It was not without an appreciable change in his dress-coat that he was ultimately rescued from the too-affectionate wall.[42]

Despite this early mishap, the New Theatre soon became an established feature of Oxford life for both Town and Gown, a vibrant symbol of the growing partnership between these ancient rivals.

Crowds on Magdalen Bridge on May morning in 1895. Some of the boys in the foreground are carrying May horns which provided a discordant and, to some listeners, an irritating contrast to the dulcet tones of the choristers on Magdalen Tower.

Cowley Road recreation ground in 1901 showing the sheep that were used to keep the grass cut. The Oxford photographer, Henry Taunt, lived opposite at 'Rivera' and complained regularly about misbehaviour on the stile leading into the field.

References

Key to Abbreviations

Bodl   Bodleian Library, Oxford
COS   Centre for Oxfordshire Studies, Central Library, Oxford
JOJ   *Jackson's Oxford Journal*
OA   Oxfordshire Archives, County Hall, Oxford
OC   *Oxford Chronicle*
OCA   Oxford City Archives, Town Hall, Oxford
OT   *Oxford Times*

1 The Setting

1   William Tuckwell, *Reminiscences of Oxford* (1900), p. 3
2   Matthew Arnold, *Poetical works* (1893), p. 282
3   T. Seccombe and H.S. Scott, *In praise of Oxford* (1910), pp. 324–5
4   Ibid., pp. 296–7
5   Edward Thomas, *Oxford* (1903), p. 247
6   A.M.M. Stedman, *Oxford: its life and schools* (1889), pp. 112–14
7   T. Seccombe and H.S. Scott, op.cit., p. 318
8   J.R. Green, *Oxford studies* (1901), p. xi
9   *OC*, 6.5.1899
10 Ibid., 20.7.1839
11 Ibid., 30.6.1838
12 Ibid., 6.6.1840
13 Ibid., 15.6.1844
14 Ibid., 2.2.1850
15 G.V. Cox, *Recollections of Oxford* (1868), pp. 370–1
16 William Tuckwell, op.cit., p. 254
17 Rhoda Broughton, *Belinda, a novel* (1883), pp. 251–2
18 Lawrence Stone, *The University in society, vol. 1* (1974), p. 91
19 D. Hunter-Blair, *In Victorian days* (1939), p. 100
20 H.W. Taunt, *Souvenir and pictorial guide to Oxford* (*c.* 1920), p. 62
21 *OT*, 3.10.1894
22 *OC*, 2.12.1882
23 J.M. Falkner, *A history of Oxfordshire* (1897), p. 314
24 Walford Davies, *Gerard Manley Hopkins: the major poems* (1977), p. 77
25 L.M. Quiller-Couch, *Reminiscences of Oxford by Oxford men* (1892), p. 367
26 T. Seccombe and H.S. Scott, op.cit., p. 769
27 Ibid., p.770

2 Academic Life

1   A.D. Godley, *Aspects of modern Oxford* (1893), p. 126
2   William Tuckwell, *Reminiscences of Oxford* (1900), p. 21
3   L.M. Quiller-Couch, *Reminiscences of Oxford by Oxford men* (1892), pp. 374–5
4   *Oxford Undergraduate's Journal*, 24.10.1866
5   L.R. Farnell, *An Oxonian looks back* (1934), pp. 72–3
6   Charles Oman, *Memories of Victorian Oxford* (1941), pp. 113–14
7   R.H. Coon, *William Warde Fowler: an Oxford humanist* (1943), p. 43
8   A.D. Godley, op.cit., pp. 108–9
9   New College Mss., Diary of H.W.B. Joseph (1895)
10 A.J. Engel, *From clergyman to don . . .* (1983), pp. 81–2
11 T. Seccombe and H.S. Scott, *In praise of Oxford* (1910), pp. 418–19
12 Jan Morris, *The Oxford book of Oxford* (1978), pp. 282–3
13 A.J. Engel, op.cit., p. 142
14 Ibid., p. 171
15 R.H. Coon, op.cit., p. 81
16 A.J. Engel, op.cit., pp. 264–5
17 A.D. Godley, op.cit., p. 70
18 Goldwin Smith, *The reorganisation of the University of Oxford* (1868), p. 3
19 Jan Morris, op.cit., pp. 281–2
20 James Pycroft, *Oxford memories, vol. 1* (1886), pp. 99–100
21 Bodl. Ms. Top. Oxon. e. 182. Mrs B. Batty, Oxford in term-time (1890)

22 A.M.M. Stedman, *Oxford: its life and schools* (1889), pp. 104–5
23 R.H. Coon, op.cit., pp. 42–3
24 Mark Pattison, *Memoirs* (1885), p. 53
25 Thomas Hughes, *Tom Brown at Oxford* (1861), p. 6
26 John Corbin, *An American at Oxford* (1902), pp. 168–9
27 C.F. Cholmondeley diary 1885–7 in possession of David Eddershaw, 10 Dunstan Avenue, Chipping Norton
28 *Autobiography of Montagu Burrows* (1908), pp. 201–2
29 Jan Morris, op.cit., pp. 280–1
30 Hilaire Belloc, *Complete verse* (1970), pp. 153–4
31 R. St J. Tyrwhitt *Hugh Heron, Christ Church* (1880), pp. 273–4
32 James Pycroft, *Oxford memories, vol. 1* (1886), pp. 88–9
33 Ibid., *The collegian's guide* (1845), p. 278
34. A.D. Godley, *Lays of modern Oxford* (1874), pp. 94–5
35 *Oxford Undergraduate's Journal,* 14.2.1866
36 Vera Brittain, *The women at Oxford* (1960), p. 18
37 Elizabeth Wordsworth, *Glimpses of the past* (1912), pp. 149–51
38 Jan Morris, op.cit., pp. 286–7; Vera Brittain, op.cit., p. 69
39 *Oxford Magazine,* 19.2.1896, 26.2.1896
40 Georgina Battiscombe, *Reluctant pioneer: The life of Elizabeth Wordsworth,* (1978), p. 132

3 Varsity Characters

1 William Tuckwell, *Reminiscences of Oxford* (1900), pp. 278–80
2 Ibid., pp. 164–6
3 Geoffrey Faber, *Jowett: a portrait with background* (1957), p. 359
4 John Corbin, *An American at Oxford* (1902), p. 181
5 C.E. Mallet, *A history of the University of Oxford, vol. 3* (1927), p. 456
6 Ibid., pp. 465–6
7 Alan Mackinnon, *The Oxford Amateurs* (1910), pp. 87–91
8 Charles Oman, *Memories of Victorian Oxford* (1941), p. 210
9 V.C.H. Green, *A history of Oxford University* (1974), p. 166
10 Rhoda Broughton, *Belinda, a novel* (1883), p. 294
11 William Hayter, *Spooner: a biography* (1977), p. 29
12 Charles Oman, op.cit., p. 93
13 *The Isis,* 18.5.1895, 28.11.1896
14 M.N. Cohen, *Lewis Carroll: interviews and recollections* (1989), p. 91
15 G.B. Grundy, *Fifty-five years at Oxford* (1945), p. 175
16 M.N. Cohen, op.cit., p. 110
17 *Complete Works of Lewis Carroll* (1939), pp. 1064–5
18 C.E. Mallet, op.cit., p. 447
19 J.J. Moore, *Oxford men and manners* (1874), p. 66
20 H.W. Taunt, The Hinkseys near Oxford (unpublished typescript), pp. 37–8
21 Ibid., p. 45
22 *British Medical Journal,* 27.10.1900
23 J.B. Atlay, *Sir Henry Wentworth Acland, Bart.* (1903), pp. 218–19
24 *British Medical Journal,* 27.10.1900
25 William Tuckwell, op.cit., p. 40
26 C.E. Mallet, op.cit., p. 224
27 William Tuckwell, op.cit., p. 40
28 T. Seccombe and H.S. Scott, *In praise of Oxford* (1910), pp. 231–2
29 William Tuckwell, op.cit., p. 53
30 Charles Oman, op.cit., pp. 204–5
31 G.B. Grundy, op.cit., p. 129
32 L.R. Farnell, *An Oxonian looks back* (1934), p. 152
33 Elizabeth Wordsworth, *Glimpses of the past* (1912), pp. 139–40
34 L.M. Quiller-Couch, *Reminiscences of Oxford by Oxford men* (1892), p. 312
35 G.B. Grundy, op.cit., pp. 81–2
36 Ibid., pp. 76–7
37 Elizabeth Wordsworth, op.cit., p. 140
38 William Hayter, op.cit., p. 36
39 E.F. Carritt, *Fifty years a don* (1960), pp. 8–9
40 G.B. Grundy, op.cit., p. 113
41 E.F. Carritt, op.cit., p. 6
42 D. Hunter-Blair, *In Victorian days* (1939), pp. 118–19
43 Ibid., p. 122
44 Christine Poulson, *William Morris* (1989), pp. 10–24
45 T. Seccombe and H.S. Scott, op.cit., p. 661
46 *Oxford Magazine,* 29.11.1956
47 William Tuckwell, op.cit., p. 39
48 T. Seccombe and H.S. Scott, op.cit., pp. 647–8
49 *Memories of some Oxford pets* (1900), p. 2

4 An Oxford Year

1 A.D. Godley, *Aspects of modern Oxford* (1893), p. 22
2 Cuthbert Bede, *The adventures of Mr Verdant Green* (1853), p. 24
3 Bodl. MS. Top. Oxon .e. 182. Mrs B. Batty, *Oxford in term-time* (1890), pp. 1–2
4 Cuthbert Bede, op.cit., p. 50
5 Jan Morris, *The Oxford Book of Oxford* (1978), p. 250
6 W.K.R. Bedford, *Outcomes of old Oxford* (1899), pp. 2–3
7 L.M. Quiller-Couch, *Reminiscences of Oxford by Oxford men* (1892), p. 307

8   T. Seccombe and H.S. Scott, *In praise of Oxford* (1910), pp. 392–3
9   Edward Thomas, *Oxford* (1903), p. 111
10 T. Seccombe and H.S. Scott, op.cit., p. 349
11 James Pycroft, *The Collegian's guide* (1845), pp. 145–6
12 Thomas Hughes, *Tom Brown at Oxford* (1861), p. 21
13 Ibid., p. 19
14 William Tuckwell, *Reminiscences of Oxford* (1900), p. 125
15 W.E. Sherwood, *Oxford yesterday* (1927), p. 26
16 Samuel Sidney, *Rides on railways* (1851), p. 47
17 G.V. Cox, *Recollections of Oxford* (1868), p. 399
18 *OC*, 8.12.1860
19 John Corbin, *An American at Oxford* (1902), pp. 132–3
20 A.M.M. Stedman, *Oxford: its life and schools* (1889), pp. 97–8
21 M.J. Gifford, *Pages from the diary of an Oxford lady* (1932), pp. 39, 61, 72–3
22 William Tuckwell, op.cit., pp. 113–14
23 A.M.M. Stedman, op.cit., p. 90
24 New College Mss., Diary of H.W.B. Joseph, 1895
25 John Corbin, op.cit., p.146
26 Alan Mackinnon, *The Oxford Amateurs* (1910), pp. 20–1
27 A.M.M. Stedman, op.cit., p. 95
28 C.F. Cholmondeley diary 1885–7 in the possession of David Eddershaw,10 Dunstan Avenue, Chipping Norton
29 John Corbin, op.cit., pp. 85–6
30 Geoffrey Bolton, *History of the OUCC* (1962), pp. 110–13
31 *The Isis*, 25.5.1895
32 T. Seccombe and H.S. Scott, op.cit., pp. 554–5
33 Edward Thomas, op.cit., p. 184
34 C.F. Cholmondeley diary, op.cit.
35 Thomas Hughes, op.cit., p. 249
36 C.S. Lucy diary 1891, copy in COS
37 *OC*, 1.7.1843
38 Ibid., 17.6.1871
39 Thomas Hughes, op.cit., pp. 267–8

5 Undergraduate Discipline

1   A.D. Godley, *Lays of Modern Oxford* (1874), p. 41
2   Charles Oman, *Memories of Victorian Oxford* (1941), pp. 171–2
3   Bodl. Ms. Top. Oxon.b. 151 University Police Report Book, 1855–7
4   A.J. Engel, ' "Immoral intentions": the University of Oxford and the problem of prostitution, 1827–1914', *Victorian Studies*, (1979/80), p. 89

5   *OC*, 17.12.1892
6   Ibid., 14.11.1874
7   Ibid., 21.11.1874
8   Thomas Hughes, *Tom Brown at Oxford* (1861), pp. 143–4
9   Mark Tellar, *A young man's passage* (1952), pp. 112–13
10 T. Seccombe and H.S. Scott, *In praise of Oxford* (1910), p. 767
11 Ibid., p. 400
12 Oxford Railway Act, 1843 (6 Victoria, cap. X)
13 John Corbin, *An American at Oxford* (1902), p. 49
14 Mark Tellar, op.cit., pp. 159–60
15 G.B. Grundy, *Fifty-five years at Oxford* (1945), pp. 54–5
16 James Pycroft, *Oxford memories, vol. 1* (1886), pp. 18–19
17 L.M. Quiller-Couch, *Reminiscences of Oxford by Oxford men* (1892), pp. 359–60
18 L.R. Farnell, *An Oxonian looks back* (1934), p. 134
19 T. Seccombe and H.S. Scott, op.cit., pp. 534–5
20 *OC*, 26.5.1894
21 Jan Morris, *The Oxford Book of Oxford* (1978), p. 269

6 North Oxford

1   T. Seccombe and H.S. Scott, *In praise of Oxford* (1910), p. 769
2   Malcolm Graham, The suburbs of Victorian Oxford Ph.D, University of Leicester (1985), pp. 59–61
3   *Oxford University and City Guide* (*c.* 1860), p. 230
4   Willliam Tuckwell, *Reminiscences of Oxford* (1900), p. 254
5   OA Ms. Top. Oxon. *c*.105, fol.182
6   *OC*, 14.10.1882
7   St John's College Mss. Est.I.F.35, 1.2.1884
8   Naomi Mitchison, *Small talk: memories of an Edwardian childhood* (1973), pp. 14–15
9   L.K. Haldane, Friends and kindred (1961), p. 155
10 Bodl. Ms. Eng. misc. e. 674, fol.13
11 Jan Morris, *The Oxford Book of Oxford* (1978), pp. 287–8
12 Georgina Battiscombe, *Reluctant pioneer: The life of Elizabeth Wordsworth*, (1978), p. 54
13 L.K. Haldane, op.cit., pp. 157–8
14 Bodl. Ms. Eng. misc. e. 674, fol.47
15 L.K. Haldane, op.cit., p. 156
16 Bodl. Ms. Eng. misc. e.677, fol.184
17 Ethel Hatch, 'Some reminiscences of Oxford', *Oxford Magazine* (1955/56), pp. 501–2
18 C.S. Lucy Diary 1884–94: copy in COS

19 Rhoda Broughton, *Belinda, a novel* (1883), p. 286
20 *OC,* 24.4.1897
21 Naomi Mitchison, op.cit., p.108
22 COS, Carmen Welch papers
23 Bodl. Ms. Eng. misc. e. 677, ff. 105, 171
24 *OT,* 5.1.1889
25 *OC,* 20.5.1882
26 St John's College Mss .Est .I.F. 34, 29.6.1882
27 Ibid., Est .I.F. 13, p. 474
28 OCA, Town Clerk's Correspondence, 1898 'M'
29 Naomi Mitchison, op.cit., p. 90
30 *OC,* 10.6.1899
31 Bodl. Ms. Top. Oxon. d 501, p. 80
32 F.M. Gamlen, *My Memoirs* (1953), pp. 15–16
33 *OC,* 6.1.1872
34 Bodl. Ms. Eng. Misc. e. 675, fol.67
35 *OC,* 7.2.1880
36 Ibid., 21.8.1897
37 Bodl. Ms. Eng. Misc. e. 697, p. 8
38 Malcolm Graham, *Henry Taunt of Oxford* (1973), p. 12

7 Employment

1 *Echoes from the Oxford Magazine* (1890), p. 7
2 Cuthbert Bede, *The adventures of Mr Verdant Green* (1853), pp. 91–2
3 James Pycroft, *The Collegian's guide* (1845), p. 237
4 *OC,* 12.2.1848
5 A.M.M. Stedman, *Oxford: its life and schools* (1889), p. 97
6 *Census of England and Wales, 1901, County of Oxford* (1903), pp. 50–1
7 John Corbin, *An American at Oxford* (1902), pp. 12–13
8 Edward Thomas, *Oxford* (1903), pp. 150–1
9 Horace Hart, *The University Press at Oxford* (1894), p. 6
10 *OC,* 17.6.1865
11 Ibid., 28.10.1876
12 C.F. Cholmondeley diary 1885–7 in the possession of David Eddershaw, 10 Dunstan Avenue, Chipping Norton
13 *OC,* 21.4.1855
14 Brigid Allen, *Cooper's Oxford: a history of Frank Cooper Limited* (1989), *passim*
15 Oxford University Archives LHD/misc/3/7
16 *JOJ,* 4.5.1861
17 Samuel Sidney, *Rides on railways* (1851), p. 34
18 Alan Crossley (ed.), *Victoria History of the County of Oxford, vol. 4* (1979), p. 216
19 *OC,* 13.11.1886, 5.2.1887, 24.12.1887
20 *Census of England and Wales, 1901, County of Oxford* (1903), p. 50
21 *OC,* 10.6.1865
22 Ibid., 14.4.1894
23 Ibid., 3.5.1873
24 Bodl. Ms. Eng. misc. e. 677, p. 187
25 *OC,* 20.5.1899
26 *Census of England and Wales, 1901, County of Oxford* (1903), p. 50
27 *OC,* 30.10.1897
28 Christ Church Mss. 78/361
29 G.V. Cox, *Recollections of Oxford* (1868), p. 429
30 *OC,* 18.6.1898
31 *OC,* 19.4.1862
32 OA, T/SL 56
33 *OC,* 10.3.1888, 25.1.1879
34 Ibid., 30.7.1881
35 Ibid., 28.1.1882
36 Ibid., 14.1.1871
37 Ibid., 1.6.1867
38 Ibid., 30.5.1896
39 Ibid., 19.2.1898
40 Ibid., 27.5.1899
41 Edward Thomas, op.cit., p. 178
42 Barbara Burke, *Barbara goes to Oxford* (1907), p. 65
43 *OT ,*4.1.1890
44 *OC,* 30.9.1899

8 Church and School

1 Willliam Tuckwell, *Reminiscences of Oxford* (1900), p. 144
2 James Pycroft, *Oxford memories, vol. 2* (1886), p. 24
3 G.V. Cox, *Recollections of Oxford* (1868), p. 338
4 *JOJ,* 19.12.1846
5 W.E. Sherwood, *Oxford yesterday* (1927), pp. 18–19
6 Bodl. Ms. Top. Oxon. d. 484. C.L.M. Hawtrey, Scrapbook of Jericho (1956), pp. 49–51
7 *OC,* 26.5.1877
8 Ibid., 15.1.1870
9 Ibid., 31.10.1868
10 J.S. Reynolds, *Canon Christopher of St Aldate's Oxford* (1967), p. 199
11 Ibid., pp. 201–2

12 Ibid., p. 286
13 D. Hunter-Blair, *In Victorian days* (1939), pp. 89–90
14 *OC,* 9.6.1877
15 Bodl. Per. G.A. Oxon 4° 120
16 *OC,* 24.9.1888
17 Ibid., 1.6.1898
18 Ibid., 15.10.1881
19 Ibid., 4.2.1865
20 E.L. Hicks, *Henry Bazely: the Oxford Evangelist* (1886), p. 133
21 *OC,* 15.10.1881
22 J.S. Reynolds, op.cit., p. 231
23 Christ Church Mss. 78/229
24 *OC,* 23.9.1882
25 Ibid., 4.2.1871
26 Malcolm Graham, The suburbs of Victorian Oxford Ph.D, University of Leicester (1985), pp. 418–19
27 *JOJ,* 6.3.1858
28 *OC,* 8.10.1864
29 Ibid., 4.1.1879
30 Ibid., 15.3.1879
31 COS, Cowley Evangelist, May 1892
32 R.L. Nettleship, *Memoir of Thomas Hill Green* (1906), pp. 80–1, 182–3
33 Malcolm Graham, op.cit., pp. 422–4
34 V.E. Stack, *Oxford High School: G.P.D.S.T., 1875–1960* (1963), pp. 1–2

9 Public Services

1 G.V. Cox, *Recollections of Oxford* (1868), p. 243
2 *Oxford Herald,* 29.7.1848
3 OCA, F.2.1., p. 57
4 W.E. Sherwood, *Oxford yesterday* (1927), p. 10
5 *OC,* 22.9.1877
6 *Report of evidence . . . sewerage, drainage and water supply* (1851), p. 57
7 *OC,* 25.8.1866
8 Ibid., 29.9.1877
9 Ibid., 21.2.1880
10 Ibid., 15.9.1883, 22.10.1887
11 *Report of evidence . . .* , op.cit., p. 51
12 Ibid., p. 55
13 *OC,* 4.5.1867
14 Ibid., 19.10.1872, 5.4.1873
15 Ibid., 27.4.1878

16 Ibid., 16.9.1854
17 Ibid., 2.7.1870, 30.7.1870
18 Ibid., 7.1.1871, 13.1.1872, 24.8.1872
19 Ibid., 9.10.1886
20 Ibid., 8.1.1887
21 OCA, R. 6.9, pp. 154–5
22 *OC* ,26.5.1866
23 OCA, Town Clerk's Correspondence 1897 'W'
24 *OC,* 5.12.1891
25 Ibid., 16.2.1867
26 St John's College Mss. Est. I.F. 31
27 *OC,* 23.11.1878, 3.12.1881, 11.2.1882
28 OCA, City Engineer's Newscutting Book, 1881–6
29 *OC,* 17.12.1881, 29.10.1881, 7.1.1882
30 *JOJ,* 26.1.1878
31 *OC,* 7.7.1883
32 Ibid., 25.6.1892
33 Hilaire Belloc, *Complete verse* (1970), p. 156
34 Bodl. Ms. Eng. misc. e. 697, pp. 7, 9
35 *OC,* 14.7.1900

10 Social Conditions

1 Thomas Hardy, *Jude the obscure* (1896), pp. 138–9
2 *Report of evidence . . . sewerage, drainage and water supply* (1851), p. 78
3 H.W. Acland, *Memoir on the outbreak of cholera . . .* (1856), p. 46
4 *OC,* 27.7.1872
5 Ibid.
6 *OC,* 31.5.1856
7 Ibid., 25.1.1873
8 Ibid., 16.12.1893
9 C.V. Butler, *Social conditions in Oxford* (1912), pp. 138–9
10 *OC,* 16.12.1893
11 Ibid., 22.12.1860
12 H.W. Acland, op.cit., pp. 47–8
13 C.J. Day, University and City (unpublished typescript), p. 14
14 *OC,* 28.11.1891
15 *JOJ,* 24.1.1875
16 Ibid., 27.8.1870
17 *OC,* 9.2.1889
18 Ibid., 11.6.1870
19 *JOJ,* 14.5.1870
20 *OC,* 22.1.1859

21 Ibid., 16.11.1867
22 Ibid., 21.9.1872
23 Ibid., 4.6.1870
24 Ibid., 9.9.1882
25 Ibid., 23.6.1877
26 *Oxford Architectural and Historical SocietyProceedings*, vol. 6 (1897), pp. 139–40
27 *OC*, 8.10.1887
28 *JOJ*, 13.10.1866, 19.10.1867; OCA R.5.3., pp. 174–5, 218
29 *OC*, 20.6.1868
30 Christ Church Mss. 78/244–5

11 Popular Recreation

1   *OC*, 17.7.1852
2   Ibid., 13.12.1862
3   *JOJ*, 21.7.1877
4   *OC*, 25.7.1896
5   Ibid., 23.10.1886
6   Ibid., 20.6.1896
7   *JOJ*, 26.6.1880
8   *OC*, 10.7.1869, 6.7.1889
9   Ibid., 17.10.1868, 12.10.1895
10 Ibid., 29.12.1860
11 Ibid., 25.1.1879
12 Ibid., 24.1.1891
13 Ibid., 12.8.1865
14 F.M. Gamlen, *My memoirs* (1953), p. 23
15 *OC*, 14.9.1889
16 Thomas Hughes, *Tom Brown at Oxford* (1861), pp. 100–1
17 *OC*, 10.8.1861
18 *JOJ*, 29.6.1861
19 *OC*, 29.10.1898
20 COS, Cowley St John Parish Magazine
21 *OC*, 17.2.1877
22 Ibid., 23.11.1878
23 Ibid., 19.10.1872
24 Ibid., 26.7.1873
25 Ibid., 1.1.1876
26 Ibid., 18.10.1856
27 *JOJ*, 27.8.1870
28 Ibid., 28.8.1852
29 Ibid., 23.7.1898

30 Malcolm Graham, The suburbs of Victorian Oxford Ph.D, University of Leicester (1985), p. 443
31 *OC*, 11.6.1892
32 Ibid., 3.8.1900
33 *Complete works of Lewis Carroll* (1939), p. 823
34 *OC*, 9.5.1896
35 Ibid., 5.11.1892
36 OCA, Town Clerk's Correspondence 1897 'T'
37 *OC*, 1.7.1899
38 Ibid., 27.10.1888
39 Ibid., 22.8.1891
40 Ibid., 19.5.1855, 8.9.1855, 15.9.1855
41 Malcolm Graham, op.cit., p. 455
42 *OC*, 24.6.1893
43 *JOJ*, 11.12.1869
44 *OC*, 1.2.1890, 18.11.1899
45 *OC*, 21.1.1888
46 Ibid., 8.4.1899

12 Town and Gown

1   Cuthbert Bede, *The adventures of Mr Verdant Green* (1853), pp. 30–1
2   T. Seccombe and H.S. Scott, *In praise of Oxford* (1910), p. 586
3   *OC*, 12.11.1859
4   T.F. Plowman, *In the days of Victoria* (1918), pp. 218–19
5   *OC*, 20.4.1872
6   Ibid., 15.5.1897
7   Ivor Thomas, *Our Lord Birkenhead: an Oxford appreciation* (1930), pp. 84–5
8   *Dark Blue*, vol. 1 (1871), pp. 371–2
9   F.M. Gamlen, *My memoirs* (1953), p. 9
10 Naomi Mitchison, *Small talk: memories of an Edwardian childhood* (1973), p. 50
11 Margaret Fletcher, *O, call back yesterday* (1939), p. 46
12 *OC*, 6.1.1877
13 Ibid., 20.1.1872
14 Ibid., 23.3.1867
15 C.J. Day, University and city (unpublished typescript), p. 9
16 *OC*, 18.11.1899
17 Christ Church Mss. 68/226
18 Ibid.
19 Ibid., 78/135
20 *OC*, 11.11.1876

21   *Dark Blue*, vol. 1 (1871). p. 371

22   *OC*, 25.12.1880

23   *Report of the Delegacy of Lodging Houses . . .1881–82* (1882), p. 17–18

24   C.J. Day, op.cit., pp. 10–13

25   *OC*, 23.12.1865

26   Brasenose College Mss. Grandpont Letters 1872–95

27   St John's College Mss. Admin. II. A.2., p. 45

28   *OC*, 17.9.1881

29   Ibid., 1.1.1876

30   John Marriott, *Memories of four score years* (1946), p. 44

31   A.G. Gibson, *The Radcliffe Infirmary* (1926), pp. 126–38

32   *OC*, 9.6.1877

33   Ibid., 4.11.1882

34   Ibid., 8.11.1877, 5.11.1881

35   Ibid., 17.10.1885, 30.4.1887

36   Ibid., 4.11.1876

37   *Autobiography of Montagu Burrows* (1908), pp. 234–5

38   *OC*, 7.8.1880

39   *JOJ*, 21.2.1880

40   *OC*, 17.11.1888

41   Alan Mackinnon, *The Oxford amateurs* (1910), pp. 41–2

42   Ibid., pp. 116–92

Picture Credits

The author and the publishers wish to thank the following for their permission to reproduce the illustrations in this book:

Bodleian Library, Oxford: 12 (Arch.k.c.4.f.55); 20 (G.A.Oxon.b.122 f.14r); 29 (G.A.Oxon.a.61(39)); 55 (G.A.Oxon.4° 861); 56 (G.A.Oxon.a.72 p. 89); 57 (MS. Top.Oxon.b.89 (14)); 72 (G.A.Oxon.a.72 p. 99); 116 (MS.Top.Oxon.d.484 p. 64); 124 (G.A.Oxon.a.53(38)); 141 (MS.Top.Oxon.d.505(48)); 147 (G.A.Oxon.4°784 f.2v). Brasenose College: 179. Christ Church: 41. Lady Margaret Hall: 33. Manchester City Art Gallery: 6. Oriel College: 26, 50, 142. Oxford City Council: 174. Oxfordshire Photographic Archive (Oxfordshire County Council Leisure & Arts, Central Library, Westgate, Oxford): 2, 8, 10-11, 13, 15-16, 18, 22, 24, 28, 31, 34, 36, 38, 40, 42-4, 48, 52, 57, 60-2, 64-5, 67, 69-71, 74-7, 81, 83-4, 86, 88-9, 91, 93, 95-6, 98-9, 101, 103-8, 110-12, 115, 117-20, 122, 126-30, 132, 134, 136-8, 140, 143, 146, 148, 150, 153-4, 157-8, 161-3, 165, 167, 170, 172, 176-7, 181-2.

Index

Figures in italic indicate illustrations.